How To Sell Yourself As An Actor

☞ **Fourth Edition**
revised and updated

© 1990, 1992, 1996, 1999, 2001 K Callan
ISBN 1-878355-10-4
ISSN Library of Congress Catalog Card Number 91-65952

Other books by K Callan:

An Actor's Workbook
The Los Angeles Agent Book
The New York Agent Book
The Life of the Party
The Script is Finished, Now What Do I Do?
Directing Your Directing Career

Illustrations: Barry Wetmore
Photography: Cap Cities ABC
Editor: Kristi Nolte

☞ Introduction

The concept of translating acting ability into gainful employment eludes many people. Most people can easily figure out how to study, learn lines and get onstage. Many, however, need help with the ABCs of actually getting a job.

How to Sell Yourself as an Actor exists not only for those folk who have never bothered with business details, but also for those who are naturally entrepreneurial with decent business skills, but would like some encouragement and/or new ideas.

At this point in my writing career, I have written and researched books for actors, writers and directors. The overview the research has given me has changed the way I look at the business.

I have a much clearer idea now of how management makes buying decisions and none of that criteria has much to do with me as a person, only as a commodity. It still hurts when I am rejected, but now that I know what goes on, I realize it really isn't personal. It's not personal when they hire me either!

When you have finished reading this book, I hope you will not only have gained knowledge and perspective, but that your brain will be open to all the other possibilities that are available in the business and in your life.

There's a real possibility that you might decide you really don't want to be an actor after you read this book. If the facts sober you now, think how much more sobering they will be after ten years of strife.

If you do decide to go on with your pursuit, you will be armed with a clear picture of the realities involved, legitimate information about what it's really like, and enough data to enter the business in an organized and intelligent way.

How to Sell Yourself as an Actor presents a way of thinking about the business that can help you retain your sense of humor, your sanity and even make you feel blessed that the spotlight is not shining on you until you have something to show.

Whatever you decide to do, start doing it now. You

are falling out of an age-range even as we speak.

You'll get the most out of this book if you read it all the way through, get the concept and then go back and read it again as you begin to formulate your plan of attack.

Good luck.

K Callan
PO Box 1612
Studio City, CA 91614
E-mail: SwedenPr@aol.com

Table of Contents

1   The Product

Many actors prefer to see their profession as art rather than business. Sometimes it is, but mostly, at a professional level, acting is about being able to make money at something most of us would do for free, if someone else would only pay our rent and buy us food. Since few of us have that luxury, teaching yourself to be businesslike is merely an extension of your acting education. Some people think actors lack the ability to be businesslike, I don't, I believe many actors just never think about it.

The financial risks and rewards of the business are so large and competition so fierce, that an actor's attention to all the facets of selling himself is crucial and may mean the difference between employment and despair.

Fifty years ago, film studios signed actors to long indentured contracts within what was called *the studio system*. Young actors of a certain look were chosen, schooled, groomed and developed by featuring them in ever larger roles until the actors graduated into starring parts either as the leading man or woman or the character lead.

The only vestiges of that day exist within the networks where actors are signed to development deals while the network seeks to have a vehicle built for the rising star as well as for performers who have already proven themselves as television draws.

The rising stars these days are most often stand up performers who have already spent entrepreneurial years creating a character and/or material that showcased them to the networks in a commercial way. Sometimes a fortunate actor whose part (large or small) in a current successful movie has garnered attention will also be the object of network's ardor.

You'll notice that I am not describing anyone

here who was just walking down the street and fell into a network contract.

Going into Business

A smart business person planning to invest time, energy, and his life savings in a new business, commits himself to relentless research. He interviews people in the field, checks the library and/or the Internet for information and conducts a market survey to see if there is a need for his product.

He identifies potential customers, checks to see how much money they have to spend, investigates what they are already buying and seeks to become a specialist in his field. He knows he will have to produce a product that is superior, unique, and/or impacts the marketplace in some new way in order to access the system.

An actor is no different than any other business person. To enter the marketplace in an effective way, the actor needs to analyze his product by coming up with clear, concise answers to a series of essential questions:

- Who am I?
- Why do I want to act?
- Where do I want to act?
- What do I have that no one else has?
- How will I go about entering the marketplace?
- Am I ready?

Who Am I?

Are you emotionally balanced? Excitable? Passive? Are you a self starter? Do you have a lot of drive? How well do you get along with people? How are you at meeting people?

Although one's physical beauty is paramount in the diverse components of your showbiz persona, your capacity to roll with the punches, change directions, be entrepreneurial and to think clearly and quickly are the qualities that will ultimately reward you with the ability to make a living as an artist.

Are you white? Black? Chicano? Indian? Male? Female? Old? Young? Beautiful? Homely?

Your visible personhood, age, race, sex and beauty, or lack of it, significantly influence how you will be received in any marketplace.

Why Do I Want to Act?

Do you want to play all the great parts? Are you excited by the process of acting or are you motivated by fame and fortune and your idea of the actor's lifestyle?

Many successful actors routinely confess in the press that they decided to act in college as a way of meeting girls. It's true, actors get more than their share of adulation from the opposite sex, but basically, that's true of all successful men and women regardless of their profession. Everyone wants to be around winners.

It's romantic to consider winning your Oscar, driving your Rolls Royce, eating at Spago, kissing beautiful co-stars, and signing autographs, but in reality, it's not fulfilling to walk around New York City every day dropping off pictures to people who not only won't open the door to receive them, but have signs posted saying specifically, *Actors, do not ring our bell.*

It's debilitating to be thought of as a necessary evil. It's heartbreaking to be 40 years old and not have a decent place to live. Being perennially unemployed damages the soul.

If you see yourself able to be happy and fulfilled in any other endeavor, do it. There is not enough money in the world to compensate for the actor's life. It has to be done for love or you will drop out along the way, bitter, and cranky over the many wasted years.

Where Do I Want to Act?

Do you plan to have a career in your own hometown or are you interested in competing in major marketplaces like New York or Los Angeles or Chicago?

Have you mined all the opportunities in your own backyard? If you are going to assault the larger marketplaces, do you know what that entails? Are you really ready to move away from home and start a totally new life with no support group?

What Do I Have That No One Else Has?

This is the really tough question. What makes you so special? If you can't find a reason (other than your deep need) then, it's going to take you a long time. If you are selling shoes and they're just like everyone else's (same price, color, quality, style) why would I want to buy yours when I already know many brands of shoes that fit me, have a style I like, the price is right and that feel great?

You must find a way to separate yourself from the pack. What is it about you that would make a director choose you over the thousands of others who are your competition? Are you prettier? Wittier? Uglier? Fatter? Thinner? Is your point of view more informed? Do you even own who you are? What do you want to communicate? You may not know the answer to this question right now, but it must be on your mind constantly for you to formulate the answer.

If you are interested in acting as a means of getting approval, forget it. For every yes vote, there will be a thousand nos.

How Will I Go About Entering the Marketplace?

Do you have any idea how to market yourself? If I told you to sit down now and write seven pages specifically entailing your game plan, could you do it? If you can't/won't write a market survey and projection for your small business, you are starting further down on the food chain than you need to.

Am I Ready?

Are you ready to start right now? Are you waiting until you are out of school? Till your kids are grown? Until you save enough money to quit your current job?

If you are going to be an actor, there are steps in your preparation that you can take as soon as the decision is clear in your mind. You may not be ready to make the leap of quitting your day job or even being in a play, but you can begin to train yourself, discipline your thinking, modify your expectations and begin to create your life.

This book is designed to help you look realistically at the profession and the kind of energy, creative thought process, and follow-through necessary to market yourself successfully.

Begin now. If you do, you can speed your journey along as well as receive the slings and arrows of a difficult life with perspective. It will still hurt to get rejected, but if you understand the rules of the marketplace, you may, in time, become able to take it less personally.

Wrap Up

✓   evaluate the marketplace
✓   analyze your product
✓   determine your game plan
✓   establish a time frame for your goals
✓   identify the uniqueness of your product
✓   understand the rules of the game
✓   create your life

2   What Are Your Chances?

One's feelings about choosing acting as a profession/lifestyle often correspond to the beginning stages of being in love: only able to see the glamorous surface, unwilling/unable to take a closer look. In all love affairs, it's difficult for the smitten to listen to the bystander dispassionately view and detail the pitfalls ahead.

I'm not a dispassionate bystander, since I've been in my own lifelong relationship with showbusiness (the most perfect dysfunctional family you can ever choose), but my own years of commitment, experience and struggle give some perspective.

As in marriage, you're not just choosing the love object, but the attendant lifestyle. Before you waste time pursuing this elusive career, consider whether or not you are suited to it.

Are you and the acting profession right for each other? Forgetting specialness and talent until later, do your sex, age, ethnic, physical and emotional package match your choice of career?

Physicality Is Destiny

Whether you like it or not, it is true that your face is your fortune. If you are Michelle Pfeiffer, Meg Ryan or Brad Pitt, your face can/will open many doors; if you are not perceived as a beauty, reviewers won't necessarily focus on your acting:

✦   *"You're really not attractive enough for daytime TV,"*
Kathy Bates was told by a soap opera casting director.
John Simon wrote in a review of Bates' performance in the
Off-Broadway production of Frankie and Johnnie in the Clair
de Lune *that "it was unfortunate her leading man should play*
opposite an actress who, even for a midnight snacker, is enormously
overweight."

Great Isn't Good Enough
Nikki Finke
Los Angeles Times/Calendar
January 27, 1991

If you study the quote above, you'll realize that John Simon (always a severe critic of less than physically perfect women) was mainly cranky because Bates was playing a romantic lead, something out of reach for those folk deemed character actors. He didn't say she wasn't a good actor, he just didn't seem to want to see her have a love life.

Sans screen love life, Bates enjoys an enviable career, playing leads (*Primary Colors, Misery, Fried Green Tomatoes,* etc.) and winning an Academy Award for her work in *Misery.* Ms. Bates is also a successful director.

There are a lot of beauties in Hollywood, and only one Kathy Bates. It's harder to carve out your niche when you don't physically fit the Hollywood beauty standard personified by Michelle, Demi and Julia, but once in, they can't get just another pretty face to replace you.

Although we are accustomed to Hollywood's severe beauty addiction it is disheartening to note that even television's irreverent *Saturday Night Live* demands beautiful women:

✦   *Another point of contention among the women of* SNL *is a perceived double standard in hiring: "Men have to be funny," they say, "while women have to be funny, young and pretty."*
     The Incredible Shrinking Women of
     Saturday Night Live
     Tom O'Neill
     Us
     December 1994

It's true in any walk of life: people who are beautiful have it easier. I, too, like to gaze at beautiful people. I find that beauty nourishes me, whether it is a beautiful day, a walk on the beach or smelling a lovely flower. This is not to say you have to be beautiful in order to work as an actor. I believe you can look like Quasimodo and have a career if you really believe in yourself and pursue your dream in a focused way.

We could debate the relative merits of being beautiful and thus being deprived of the struggle to prove oneself. Joanne Woodward enjoyed a successful career with multiple Academy Award nominations. Her more beautiful husband, Paul Newman, became a superstar and was only rewarded for his excellent work by an Academy Award very late in his career.

The reality that the beautiful one will probably never be developed to his/her full potential on other levels doesn't matter. Beauty wins.

So Do Men

Since films, plays, and television reflect the world surrounding us, it is no surprise that there is more opportunity for any man to work than any woman.

As a member of the Academy of Motion Picture Arts and Sciences, I am privileged to attend screenings of films eligible for consideration for the Academy Awards. Every year, a majority of films (usually action films) feature 25 to 30 men in a cast with possibly two women, frequently both of whom are blonde, beautiful, 18 and naked.

The 1998 Screen Actors Guild Report: Casting the American Scene: Fairness and Diversity in Television states:

◆ *Women consistently play one out of three roles in prime time television. Their representation increased only 3.5% since 1993. They fall short of majority even in daytime serials. They age faster than men, and as they age they are more likely to be portrayed as sexless and evil.*

1998 Screen Actors Guild Report: Casting the American Scene: Fairness and Diversity in Television:
George Gerbner
Bell Atlantic Professor of Telecommunication
Temple University, Philadelphia
December 1998

Women In The Marketplace

Bette Midler is another talented actress who doesn't fit into the mold and therefore has always had to generate her own work. Some of the films she and partner Bonnie Bruckheimer's production company, All Girl Productions, have put together are *The Rose, Beaches, Ruthless People, Outrageous Fortune,* and *Big Business.*

✦   *After* The Rose *which did good business and brought Midler a 1979 Academy Award nomination, not a single job came her way.*
   "Being a female production team is a real tribute to both of them," observes Robert Cort, who is working with them on Iris Dart's, Show Business Kills. *"This town is a boys' club, so they start at the back of the end, instead of on the 20-yard line."*
   Midler and Bruckheimer refuse to cry victim, however. "Disney treated us as bad as [it does] everybody else," quips Bruckheimer. But in Hollywood, as in the rest of life, gender inevitably factors in. As the first women to penetrate that studio's production ranks, they were grateful for a deal that gave them office space but no capital.
   For the Girls
   Elaine Dutka
   The Los Angeles Times
   July 16, 1995

Meryl Streep took a lot of heat for complaining that women are not paid as much as men for the same jobs, and though women are still not on a par with men, their salaries are expanding.

✦   *While the best-paid actresses (those who have cracked the $10 million mark) still lag behind their male counterparts — who are now working on the $20 million mark — women's salaries have become a force to contend with. Agency upheaval, supply and demand, and the fact that women are finally opening pictures are the oft-cited reasons for this above-the-line affirmative action.*

  ...Michelle Pfeiffer's Dangerous Minds *took in $14.9 million on its opening weekend. And Julia Roberts can most likely take credit for the $11.1 million opening of* Something to Talk About.

  H'wood Finally Opening Vault to Female Stars
  Andrew Whindes
  Daily Variety
  December 5, 1995

Cher takes the whole situation philosophically:

✦   *I'm not into that thing about women and films. It's hard for women anywhere. Hollywood is no different. I get paid more money than I could possibly imagine. I'm a woman and I make tons of money. I don't make as much as a man, but that's just the way it's set up. That's the reality of the way we live, but we still get paid an unbelievable amount of money to do what we would all do for nothing.*

  The Cher Conundrum
  Hilary De Vries
  The Los Angeles Times
  November 3, 1991

Who Makes the Money?

Leading men make the money. That usually means *white* leading men. Leading women make money, but not as much and not for as long. If you are an entrepreneur like Jodi Foster or Barbra Streisand, you can actually become powerful and have a career that spans generations, but that is rare. Sad to say, women's lib notwithstanding, women still are considered ornamental or less. They are condescended to rather than respected.

Character men and women can make good money in television, but Billy Baldwin will never make as much money as Alec Baldwin.

Aging and Women

No matter what profession you are in, aging is a bitch. No one wants to know you. Here you are with a brain that still thinks it's 30 and packaging that says otherwise. Women seem to have it worst of all, though. Jessica Lange is just one of the actresses who has been forced to come to grips with it:

✦ *"Aging is a big deal for a woman, and nothing prepares you for it," Lange says. "Now that I'm in my mid-40s I've thought about this a lot, and I honestly don't know why it is that a 50-year old woman is still seen as sexual and desirable in Europe but in American she's an invisible person."*

"So sure, I've said to myself, 'OK, maybe a little facelift,' but I think you just can't give in to that because if you do, you're buying into everything that's self-destructive."

Steeled Magnolia
Kristine McKenna
Los Angeles Times/Calendar
March 19, 1995

Actress Dorothy Lyman, best known for her years playing on *Mama's Family,* has found another way to cope, but she says it still hurts:

✦ *"I knew Hollywood could be cruel to women, but I never thought it would happen to me," Lyman, 48, said recently from her Hollywood Hills home. "I always thought I was too gifted an actress to be out of work. I guess I thought I was different."*

"I'm too talented to play nothing but social workers, nurses and mothers," Lyman said. "But that's about all Hollywood has to offer a middle-aged actress. It can age an intelligent person fast."

...Her pain has been softened by the discovery of new talents. A few lessons with her son's word processor helped Lyman

complete an ambitious script about the frustrations of an aging feminist. Her play, A Rage in Tenure, *ran at Theater Geo in Hollywood after receiving strong reviews.*

> Smiling Beyond Her Apocalypse
> Eric Shepard
> *Los Angeles Times*
> July 24, 1995

In addition to her success as a playwright, during most of its successful run, Lyman was resident director of *The Nanny*, a show starring and written by another entrepreneur, Fran Drescher.

It's No Picnic for Men, Either

Even if you are a member of the preferred group, age exacts its toll. When Robert DeNiro complains about age and availability of parts, you know things are bad:

✦ *Now, at 50, after 39 pictures, he is aware that age can be an obstacle. "The whole thing," he says, "is for younger people who are sexy and youthful."*

> Robert De Niro
> Elizabeth Kaye
> *The New York Times Magazine*
> November 14, 1993

You're 20 or 30 and you are reading this and you (like Dorothy Lyman) think it could never happen to you. It can. It will. You need to consider career longevity as you make your game plan.

Age/Process Time

Years ago I read an illuminating interview with one of Los Angeles' most powerful casting directors, Lynn Stalmaster. Lynn has a great eye and started many young actors on the road to stardom. One of his finds was Richard Dreyfuss.

Lynn called him in to audition for several projects, before Dreyfuss connected. Instead of giving up on Dreyfuss and scratching him from his audition lists, Lynn just said, *Richard isn't ready yet,* and continued calling him in to read until he finally scored the part that gave him the beginning of a career, *American Graffiti.*

If you did not know her story, you might think that Anne Heche (*Wag the Dog, Donnie Brasco, Six Days, Seven Nights*) simply walked into town and started working. Far from it:

✦   *"I tried out for* Carlito's Way,*" she said, "and I was too young, too green, and Pacino said, 'Give yourself four years to grow into yourself' and four years later I got* Donnie Brasco.*"*
Anne Heche Waits to Find Out if She's Still a Star
Bernard Weinraub
The New York Times
April 3, 1998

Those stories clarify for me what process is. To me, it's like conceptualizing an actor, writer, singer or director as a cake that's baking in the oven. All the ingredients are there, they just need to be cooked properly. Richard and Anne just weren't done yet.

So the process or cooking time for every actor is different. You don't want to rush things. Let the process happen.

With this thought in mind, consider age, process and my friend, John. John has not worked steadily enough for the last several years to support himself as an actor, so he has a day job. In his fifties, John finally decided that he was going to make something happen in his life. He wanted a shot at being a director. Since the prescribed route to visibility for a director is a short film, John wrote, produced and directed a short film. He asked me to look at his film. I did. It was a decent first effort.

After all the time, energy, money and love he expended on his film, John was angry that no one seemed interested in it and blamed it on the fact that he was 50 and people were holding that against him. What he didn't understand is the very logical way that the business works: If a 20-year-old produced the same movie, an agent or a producer might look at that film and say, *Hmm...promising* and keep an eye on John. A 20-year-old wouldn't expect to be hired immediately, he would know that he was on a beginning journey.

John the 50-year-old, on the other hand, expects that his 25-30 years in the business count for something and they do. He is pretty good at directing the actors; unfortunately he hasn't been learning all the other camera and crew lessons that only time and experience teach a director.

That same scenario holds true for a 50-year-old actor trying to enter the business. Not only is your cake not nearly done, but your competition already has experience in acting and getting along with people and they probably have a long list of credits as well. You'd have to be pretty terrific and quite unique to be chosen over those with proven track records.

So it's not wrinkles and sags and bags that casting directors hold against older actors entering the market-place, it's the fact that their cakes are going to need much more baking time.

Age/Demographics

Surely you've heard ad nauseam how the preferred audience age for television is 18-49. Some people call it ageism and threaten legal action, but what is perceived as ageism is simply a realistic product adjustment related to the economics of the marketplace.

I spoke with Barbara Brogliatti, Senior Vice-President of World Wide Television Publicity for Warner Bros. about why those of us over 50 are perceived as a less desirable audience by advertisers and studio heads than those in the coveted 18-49 year old demographic:

✦   *The major assumption is that by the time people are 50-60*

*years old, they have already established their favorite brands: they've
established their favorite toothpaste, their favorite soap, they're either
Pepsi drinkers or Coke drinkers.*

*If their income has risen, they might choose a different car,
but people with the more expensive cars don't do the bulk of their
advertising on television. They advertise mostly in magazines which
reach a narrower audience.*

*Cable is narrow casting. A limited amount of people will
target 50+, so that's for cable. Broadcasting is supposed to be
broad. In order to have those big budgets, you have to aim for a
large number of people. You need mass appeal. Cable is not unlike
magazines.* One of the largest magazines in the world is Modern
Maturity, *but they still have many fewer subscribers than* TV
Guide, *which has the largest circulation.*

Modern Maturity *makes a good living even though they
have 50% or fewer of the population.*
  Barbara Brogliatti, Senior Vice-President
  World Wide Television Publicity, Warner Bros.

Since it's human nature to be interested in people
like yourself, that means all those people who supposedly
have not yet made up their minds between Coke and
Pepsi (18-49) will be more receptive to making choices
while they are watching stories and listening to music that
deals with their fellow undecideds. Those of us already in
the know will have to make do with the knowledge that
although we are not the coveted group, at least we know
who we are and what we want.

Well, that's television. Brogliatti didn't say
anything about films. Perhaps the film companies care
about those unfortunates over 49.

✦ *It holds true for film. The most money made in films is
made by repeat business — kids and teens. People who are 50 or
more either like it or don't like it, they usually don't see it twice.*
On Golden Pond *was a phenomenon. That kind of exception is
not what the movie business is built on.*

*At Warner Bros., they have established, both in television
and features, a policy of trying to appeal to all demographics, even*

the less popular ones.

You'll see in the films that come from Warner Bros., not only Batman, *but stories that are family-centered* (The Little Princess) *or films that are controversial or may not make a lot of money. The less profitable projects have* Batman *to subsidize them.*

In order to do all the dramas that we do, we have to have the comedies to pay for it. This company has established itself in diversity. They have made a decision, "Okay, so our profit margin, instead of being 10, our profit margin will be 1." A lot of companies don't have that luxury. More studios keep their menus less diverse and go for the home run. We are a studio that likes to go for singles, doubles and triples, both in television and film.

Barbara Brogliatti, Senior Vice-President
World Wide Television Publicity, Warner Bros.

Beth Hymson-Ayer, president of the Casting Society of America (CSA), is on the cutting edge of the decision-making process of who gets to audition. Her perspective on the changing face of the business made me feel hopeful.

✦ *There's always been a youth-oriented audience, though before adults had the purse strings. But as the baby boomers get older, we may come full circle to a more adult market — 19 to 42 may shift to 35 to 60.*

Beth Hymson-Ayer
Cindy Mulkern
The Hollywood Reporter
November 4, 1998

I've spent a lot of space here talking about aging because I think it is important to understand the reason that actors in the preferred age group will work more and earn more than those who are older. If you are in the preferred age group, know what the future brings and plan for it.

If acting is a young person's game (and it seems to be), we should all prepare to have another career at a later stage of our lives, so that instead of having it foisted upon us, we can embrace the chance to diversify.

That's not to say we're all going to be put to death on our 50th birthdays; there will be jobs for some. There are jobs in theater, on the networks and on cable, but the employment possibilities for most of us will never equal what they were in the prime earning years of 20-40 just as in almost any other business.

Is it Possible to Make a Living Acting?

Well, yes, but it is difficult. According to the Screen Actors Guild's 1997 records, 27.5% of their 91,000 members made no money at all in that year and 40% of their members made less than $3,000. If you do the math, you'll find that only 33% made over $3,000. No figures were available for those members making $25,000 and $50,000, but only 2.8% made over $100,000 and only 1.4% made over $200,000. Since 67% of the membership doesn't even make $3,000, it's safe to say that most members of the guild find themselves unable to live solely on the money they earn as actors.

✦   *An estimated 80% of SAG's members make less than $10,000 year from acting.*
      Hollywood's 2 Major Actors' Unions Consider Merging
      Jeff Leeds
      The Los Angeles Times
      December 16, 1998

65% of the members report working only one or two SAG jobs per year, with five or fewer days on the set, while 70% supplement their performance income in a wide range of jobs, including writing, photography and teaching.

Many members own their own businesses. Older performers often work as acting teachers. Women tend to work in modeling, retail establishments, offices and restaurants; while men are more inclined to work as skilled laborers or office workers.

SAG Members Earning 1997
- 27.5 % earned no money at all
- 39.5% earned $1 to $3,000
- 2.8% earned $100,000 +
- 1.4% earned $200,000 +

New Yorkers find most of their supplemental income in the legitimate theater, bars and restaurants; while West Coast performers earn more in office positions and film support services.

Generally, young white men work more and earn more than women, minorities and those over 40.

Still sure you want to do this?

Minorities

These statistics do not take into consideration the even smaller number of jobs available to actors who are not perceived as people who could have come from Nebraska or Iowa. Being ethnic (visibly Jewish, Italian, Hispanic, Asian, etc.) cuts down on your employment opportunities.

It's only in the recent past that *black is beautiful* as far as making a living in show business. There are an increasing number of black actors who are becoming hot at the box office. Will Smith is gold. Samuel L. Jackson is hot. Morgan Freeman, Danny Glover, Laurence Fishburne and Wesley Snipes are respected. Denzel Washington had billing over Gene Hackman in *The Crimson Tide*. James Earl Jones always works. Angela Bassett got nominated for an Academy Award for *What's Love Got to Do with It?* Television shows such as *Moesha* and *Under One Roof* feature black casts. Arsenio Hall is no longer extremely visible, but he is producing and readying his next move.

Although Hollywood has finally produced some black actors who are box office, I can only think of two black women who have made the trek to superstardom in the business — Whoopi Goldberg and Oprah Winfrey. Goldberg is an international superstar and Winfrey was voted the most powerful person in show business in 1998.

Though talented and an Academy Award nominee for *The Color Purple*, Winfrey's megasuccess has come about because her own entrepreneurial skills made her visible on her Chicago talk show which drew Spielberg's attention in the first place. That show was the nucleus of the successful show which she produces and stars in today.

Many have forgotten that Whoopi Goldberg was a stand-up comedienne before her one-woman Broadway show took New York by storm. Just like Oprah, Whoopi's entrepreneurial skills put her in a position for Spielberg to propel her career forward by casting her in *The Color of Purple* as well.

Whoopi has crossed many hurdles:

◆   *Whoopi Goldberg is the only woman whose name on a comedy project will flip open bankers' wallets posthaste, to the tune of $20 million for two Buena Vista films.*

Among the high scoring women, though, Goldberg continues to be most remarkable in the international marketplace. "She's fascinating because she breaks through three major barriers internationally," notes sales veteran Kathy Morgan of Kathy Morgan International. "She's a female superstar in a man's world, when women stars tend to be these very sexy Sharon Stone types. She's an African-American actor who is strongly accepted outside the U.S., which is rare. And she's comedic, when the old saying goes that comedians don't travel overseas. She's a very unusual superstar."

Who Says Hollywood Is Politically Correct?
James Ulmer
Daily Variety
May 9, 1995

Black actresses refuse to indict color when

complaining about the lack of job opportunities. Charlayne Woodard had an impressive New York theater resume when she made the trek to Los Angeles:

✦ *"When I moved to Los Angeles and went to the first auditions, I thought I would slit my wrists. The mistake that I made was that I complained a lot. The problem here hasn't been a surfeit of work, but a dearth of the right stuff. Rarely do you get something that makes you say, 'I have to work on this,'"* says Woodard. *"The roles for me that are wonderful are so few and far between, and they tend to cast the same people over and over again."*

And though the roles are even fewer for actresses of color, Woodard is loath to blame it on race. *"One thing I have never done is that thing of saying that 'because I'm black, this is not given to me,'"* she says. *"I always feel that being an African-American woman is an asset and that's what I take into my meetings."*

What's unusual about Woodard is not her predicament, but her remedy. I said, *"No more lamentations, Charlayne. Create for yourself. Join your theater groups. That's the thing that drives you to write".*

"I will never stop doing theater. Never. The new challenge is, 'Can I make a living in film and television?' It's a different animal altogether. And I've stopped beating that animal. You've got to get on it and ride it."

A Living Work in Progress
Jan Breslauer
Los Angeles Times/Calendar
August 21, 1994

Morgan Freeman agrees that color may well not be the problem:

✦ *"Contrary to popular belief,"* he says, *"Hollywood is not necessarily race conscious. It's money conscious."*

Writing a New A-List
David Ehrenstein
Los Angeles Times/Calendar
November 12, 1995

Eriq LaSalle became a star in the acclaimed television series, *ER*. Just like the rest of us, though, he has suffered his share of hard knocks and made decisions as a result of them. Cast in the feature, *Love Field*, he was fired supposedly because he was too young to play Michelle Pfeiffer's lover.

✦   *That made no sense to me whatsoever. I said to myself, 'This is the career you have chosen. You are going to be subject to this type of thing for the rest of your career.'*
     That's when I went and took a film class in New York, just for a summer, because I definitely had to have more control over my journey. I'm one of those people who always tries to find something good out of a bad situation.
     ...This thing with Love Field *forced me to realize you better start preparing for something, just to have more control.*
     When Race Isn't a Factor
     Susan King
     Los Angeles Times/TV Times
     August 27, 1995

Mentoring

The African American factor in show business grows daily and a lot of the credit goes to those in the community who have already made strides and now seek to open the door for others.

✦   *The doors of opportunity that allowed an unprecedented number of black actors in the industry swing both ways. That is why, in recent months, a group of African Americans who made it though the door has been meeting in a rented Hollywood rehearsal space. They want to make sure that they not only manage to stay inside, but also make their presence felt.*
     They range in age from their early-20s to their mid-30s. Most of them are actors, but some want to write or produce. Some are unknown, but others are familiar faces such as Tempest Bledsoe (Cosby), *Tisha Campbell* (Martin *and* House Party *movies), Kelly Williams* (Family Matters) *and Chris Spenser* (Vibe).

What unites them is dedication to their art and the help and good graces of Bill Duke.

The actor and director of such films as A Rage in Harlem *and* Sister Act 2: Back in the Habit *has become a godfather of sorts for a segment of young Hollywood that is still finding its way.*

Boot Camp, Hollywood Style
Eric Harrison
The Los Angeles Times
November 1, 1998

Duke was challenged to start the group by actress Lalanya Masters when they sat next to each other at an awards dinner and lamented that young African Americans were not living up to the examples set by earlier generations. That discussion led to the formation of a group focused on the criteria set by Duke: the group had to concentrate on the business side of entertainment as well as the acting.

✦   *Once he started the boot camp, he required that everyone read* Daily Variety *and* The Hollywood Reporter *as well as plays by Shakespeare, Tennessee Williams, Arthur Miller and August Wilson. He also assigned books:* An Empire of Their Own, *about how immigrant Jews built the American film industry;* The Highwaymen *which profiles communications moguls; and* Megatrends, *which forecasts and examines social, economic and political trends. And he brought in prominent entertainment figures such as Denzel Washington, John Singleton and Reginald Hudlin to speak of their experiences.*

Boot Camp, Hollywood Style
Eric Harrison
The Los Angeles Times
November 1, 1998

Actor-director, Eugene Williams and producer Marceil *Hollywood* Wright hold a monthly opportunity night called *Doboy's Dozens* to provide networking opportunities for people in every area of the business.

Although the crowd (usually about 350) is predominantly black (85%), that leaves 15% of everybody else who would also like to meet and shmooze.

Williams furnishes the place with bean bag chairs and blow-up couches to give the place an aura of informality that he says leads to an egalitarian atmosphere where visible blacks like John Singleton and Bill Duke, who routinely show up, are treated the same as you and me.

The evening consists of short films on ½ inch VHS, music videos, trailers and a deejay, and is a regular meeting place for people in the community to discover and be discovered. There is plenty of time to hang out and leave your picture and resume on the table if you are an actor looking for an opportunity.

Williams also gives door prizes so you have the chance to win acting lessons, scriptwriting software or a new set of headshots in addition to the rewards of just mixing with your fellow artists.

Eugene says *get there early* or at least on time as they usually reach their limit of 350 and have to turn people away.

Doboy's Dozens
Regency West
3339 W 43rd Street (3 blocks E of Crenshaw)
Los Angeles, CA 90062
213-292-5143
E-mail: Doboydozen@aol.com
Last Wednesday of the month
$10 admission

Doboy's Dozens Film Submissions
1525 N Cahuenga Blvd. #39
Los Angeles, CA 90028
323-293-6544 for information regarding film format.

All the mentoring and networking is paying off for black men

✦   *Black males — not females — are cast in higher numbers than their share of the U.S. population.*
SAG: TV Not Plugged in to
Realities of the Poor, Disabled.
David Robb
The Hollywood Reporter
December 22, 1998

Black Talent News

Black Talent News debuted in 1995 and has now grown to include a powerful web presence as well. *Black Talent News* bills itself as *the leading source of industry news and career information by, on and for African Americans in the entertainment industry.*

Each issue details casting notices, production charts and industry news. Subscriptions are $23.97 for one year (12 issues) or $42.97 for two years (24 issues).

Black Talent News is also the founding and presenting sponsor of the *Hollywood Black Film Festival* held annually in February at USC School of Cinema-Television and the neighboring Flagship Theaters.

Black Talent News
1620 Centinela Ave., Suite 204
Inglewood, CA 90302
310-348-3944, fax 310-348-3949
E-mail: info@blacktalentnews.com
website: www.blacktalentnews.com

Hispanics

Though the situation may seem bleak when you are black and looking for a job, blacks are much better off than Hispanics:

✦   *Hispanic characters are shown less than one-third as much as their proportion of the U.S. population: They number 10.7% of*

*the U.S. but played only 2.6% of the characters on primetime TV
and 3.7% in daytime.*

Study says TV Edits Women, Minorities Out
Nick Madigan
Daily Variety
December 22, 1998

One reason Hispanics are so disenfranchised is
that they are not as organized as the African American
community and another is economics:

✦　　*Money drives decisions in Hollywood, and advertisers won't
back Latino programs on the major U.S. networks because they
can reach most of the nation's twenty-six million Latinos for less
than half the price by advertising on Spanish-language TV.*

*Dolores Kunda, Vice-President and account director for the
Leo Burnett USA Hispanic Unit in Chicago, whose clients include
Kellogg's, McDonald's and United Airlines, says "Many big
advertisers sell to moms, and the moms are watching Spanish-
language TV.*

*"If you try to market the younger Generation X Hispanic,
the question is 'how fine do you want to split up your media
dollars?' A lot of advertisers are already getting that consumer
through the Spanish-language market."*

*A recent study by A. C. Nielson seems to confirm that
notion: more than 40% of U.S. Latinos speak Spanish at home
meaning that the English-language Latino audience really consists
of no more than about fifteen million potential viewers. "It would get
me into big trouble to say this," says the leader of one Latino group,
"but once you subtract the Latinos who are Spanish-dominant, the
theory of a fractionalized market is correct. I don't blame the
studios or the networks."*

Whoa Nelly
Jill Stewart
Buzz Magazine
June/July 1995

Though things may look bleak for Latinos on
television, things are looking up in film:

✦   *While American Hispanic actors are far from being as*
bankable as their white counterparts — they're making headway
by headlining in several Hollywood offerings, including New Line's
My Family *with Edward James Olmos, Jimmy Smits and Esai*
Morales. *They can also find some comfort in the success of one of*
their Hispanic brothers, Antonio Banderas, who stars opposite
Stallone in Assassins *in a role that wasn't even written for an*
Hispanic — a good sign of mainstream penetration. Once you have
a Latino actor breaking ground in mainstream American movies, it
can have a coattail effect for the American Hispanics here, notes
agent Emanuel Nunez.

Who Says Hollywood Is Politically Correct?
James Ulmer
Daily Variety
May 9, 1995

Research Your Employment Opportunities

Where are the jobs that are right for you? Find out
by spending every evening for a month in front of the
television set with a paper and pencil. Assuming you were
trained and in the right place at the right time, are there
parts for you? On commercials? On nighttime television?
On daytime television? As you research the marketplace,
you will begin to get a true idea of how or whether you
can fit into the marketplace in a way that will enable you
to make a living.

Assess carefully who you are physically and the
impact this has on your earning power. Men who are
extremely tall and have any natural grace and athletic
ability are recruited to be basketball players. If you are a
gifted athlete who yearns to be a basketball star, but are
only five feet tall, all the heart and determination in the
world isn't going to make you into Larry Bird.

This applies to actors as well. Look at yourself.
Will you physically fit into a casting niche in the business?
Consider yourself in relation to the people who are
working: are you the right age? Do you need to be older
to logically sell who you are? If you do, don't starve while

you age, there are alternatives.

I was conducting a seminar in New York when an offbeat, not traditionally attractive, 30ish man came up and spoke to me. He had a job in local television in Connecticut and had been considering making the move to the big marketplace in New York City. Until the seminar, he had not really analyzed the fact that he is a character man who has not yet grown into himself and that he will be more physically employable in 15 years. Since he's already employed in the business, he decided to continue growing into himself where he is and postpone the move to New York until his visual age catches up to his presence.

I read an interview with Geraldine Page when she was nominated for an Academy Award for *The Pope of Greenwich Village*. She had spent the previous several years totally unemployable. She said: *I don't know who it is that has finally decided it's okay for me to work again.*

In fact, she had just been through a growth period where she was changing from one type to another, visually.

Cinematic Age

I recently spoke to a friend of mine who is a very successful actress who was preparing for a new film and was in the midst of makeup tests. My friend is 59 years old and looks great. In the film, she plays a 62-year-old woman.

In trying to make her look 62, the makeup men applied a latex film to her face. She told them it was ridiculous. In three years, she would *be* 62. She won't look that different. All the people she knows that are 62 look at least 10 years younger than the age the makeup men created.

The makeup department explained that, cinematically, people expect a 62-year-old person to appear a particular way. If you are a 62-year-old person who announces you have a 35-year-old son and a 15-year-old granddaughter and people say, *You look so young, we'd never know it*, the movie going public isn't going to buy it, either.

What They See Is What They Get

When I first went to New York, I made a lot of money in commercials. There were several reasons why I was successful, not the least of which was my Midwestern American face, a gift from my parents for which I can take no credit.

As successful as I was in New York in commercials, when I moved to Los Angeles, that particular success did not translate. In Los Angeles, they prefer prettier people. I was perfect as a *real* person in New York. In Los Angeles, reality is not the strong suit.

Because I was on the crest of an age category change, I did fewer commercials in Los Angeles. No longer the mother of young kids, I was moving into *Mother of the Bride* territory. Not only are there not that many parts for *MOB*s, there were other *MOB*s more securely in that age range, who were cinematically better able to fill that role. Interestingly, this image problem did not interfere with my film and television career during that period. Go figure.

Actors pass through many age ranges during their careers. Some will be lucrative. Others dismal. Because of age and overexposure, everything can stop without warning. One day you are doing great, finally heaving a sigh of relief, *Oh, boy, it's going to work out. I'm not going to have to worry for a while.*

And then it's over for 6 months, or a year, or a year and a half. I don't know a single actor who has been in the business for any length of time who has not had this experience. I've been told that *no young, excited actor is going to believe this will ever happen to him* and I do agree that I might not have believed it either. But no one ever told me about age ranges and changes.

When I faced this challenge for the first time, it

was painful. You think that it's all over, that you'll never work again, and that it's never happened to anyone, but you. It would have helped a bit if I had been able to say, *I never believed it would happen, but at least, I know it's part of the process and not just me. Now, I believe.*

Jimmy Cota, one of the partners of the prestigious Artists Agency in Los Angeles, put it this way:

✦   *Look at the business. A growing number of shows; the magazine shows, the reality shows, and game shows don't use actors. Sitcoms use only one or two guest stars. The amount of money available to the community is somewhat diminished. What you have is a number of people who were able to make a living who can no longer make a living. The movies are all youth-market movies with 16-17 year old kids. Once they're 23 and can no longer play seniors in high school anymore, the business slows down for them.*

Jimmy Cota
The Artists Agency/Los Angeles

✦   *Increasingly, the networks are choosing cut-rate, quasi-news shows such as* Hard Copy, Worst Disasters Ever, *or* Cops *over costly dramas. Once dominant in prime time, dramas account now for only about 30% of the program schedule.*

Too Costly for Prime Time
John Lippman
The Los Angeles Times
March 22, 1992

Emotional Strength

Do you have the temperament to withstand the stress of constant unemployment and daily rejection? New York agent, Jerry Hogan, told me he began his career as an actor, but stopped when he realized his nature couldn't handle constant rejection. The wear and tear on his ego was too much.

Of course, I contend that actors do not really go into acting because they are necessarily in their right minds. My theory is we are all drawn to this business because we come from a background of real or imagined rejection. We are, therefore, familiar with the feeling and have ways of coping with it. If we are lucky, we get healthier along the way. Sometimes we stay in the business because we are making more money than we could make anyplace else. And sometimes we leave.

Wrap Up

✓ physicality is destiny
✓ white men make the money
✓ women work considerably less after age 40
✓ research the marketplace for jobs for your type
✓ real age not synonymous with cinematic age
✓ reality-based shows cutting into actors' jobs
✓ emotional strength is vital

3   There's No Place Like Home

The biggest centers of film and television employment are, of course, Los Angeles, New York and Chicago. More filming takes place in the Los Angeles area in a day than occurs in most other cities in a year.

Even though the perennial refrain, *Broadway is dying* continues, New York is still the consummate theater town. Chicago is also a viable working environment for actors in theater and in film.

You might be surprised, however, to find the amount of work that is scattered across the land in all areas of show business.

A friend of mine, a visible working actress finally packed it in and moved home to Oregon to raise her daughter in the same kind of environment in which she grew up. Since that move, she's worked many more jobs than she had in the past three years in Los Angeles in both film and television that were shooting on location in her area.

She doesn't make as much money per show as she did in LA, but those days at scale plus 10% add up and the pleasure of working at her craft has produced a happier lifestyle than she had in Los Angeles. It doesn't cost as much to live in Oregon, either.

In the late 1950s, there was a television show called *Route 66* which shot all around the country. When they came to my hometown to shoot, as an actress with solid local credits, I was immediately called in to audition and more than elated to get (as my parents termed it) *a real acting job with Hollywood people.* I'm sure I'm not the only one who got to qualify for my Screen Actors Guild card in my own hometown on network television as a result of that show.

Although at that point in my life I thought I was going to spend the rest of my life as a homemaker in Dallas, that experience certainly gave me the idea that I might have something to sell in the larger marketplace.

The validation made it easier to have the courage to make the big move to New York when my life changed.

Where the Work Is

The latest available film location statistics published in the *Locations Survey Special Issue* by *The Hollywood Reporter* in February 1998 show that California had 510 film starts and 73,666 production days of work.

The next busiest market for film that listed its days (New York, for instance, did not) were Minnesota and New Jersey. Since some states listed only production days and not preproduction, it's difficult to make an accurate assessment regarding the top states after California.

✦　*About ⅔ of the dramatic series shown on TV are produced in California, while sitcoms are primarily produced on Hollywood sound stages. Indeed, while California doesn't track the state's number of TV production days, it represents 85% of the episodic TV market. And while the number of New York's TV production days were unavailable, sitcoms* Spin City *and* Cosby *and drama series* Law & Order *and* New York Undercover *were shot in the Empire State last year.*

> *By Production Days*
> The Editors
> *The Hollywood Reporter*
> February 7, 1997

In addition to Los Angeles, San Diego is establishing itself as a television series location alternative:

✦　*Behind Los Angeles and New York, San Diego ranks third in the country for TV series filming.*
　　Recent TV series and movies of the week shot in San Diego include The Tiger Woods Story, What Love Sees, Down, Out & Dangerous, Silk Stalkings *and* 1,000 Men and a Baby.

Unsolved Mysteries, The NFL Super Bowl *and* Good Morning America *have also hit town recently.*

Big Business
Ron Donoho
The Hollywood Reporter
November 20, 1998

The Hollywood Reporter goes on to say that television commercial production revenues are also spread into other markets besides Los Angeles and New York. Michigan, for instance matched New York in numbers of days shooting (4,000), mainly on the strength of the presence of the automotive industry.

But being in New York and/or Los Angeles might not be the best place for you. An article in the *Screen Actors Guild* magazine celebrated Nick Searcy, an actor who only got work when he left New York:

✦   *I lived in New York City for seven years, working on stage, but not on film. I never got a film acting job until I moved back to North Carolina in 1989. After a few small parts in films like* Days of Thunder *and* Love Field, *I read for a small part in* Fried Green Tomatoes *and (director) Jon Avnet thought I looked mean and stupid so he read me for the larger part of Frank Benneett.*

I got that role, and I count that as the point when my career was launched. I have had no other job but acting or directing since then. If it had not been for the North Carolina market, I would never have gotten the shot at the role in Fried Green Tomatoes.

Who Says You Have to Live in Hollywood or the Big Apple to Catch Your Rising Star?
Julie Balter
Screen Actor
November 1998

The Big Apple and the Big Orange

Who cares about the larger marketplace? If you

are sitting in Des Moines, Iowa or Avon, Montana, you may feel New York/Los Angeles considerations don't apply to you. You're not trying to get a job on *ER* or star in Oliver Stone's next movie, so what does that have to do with you? Everything. What happens in the larger marketplace is reflected across the land. Commercials cast in Oklahoma City reflect commercials cast in Manhattan. NY/LA commercials follow trends set by current films and set trends for the rest of the nation.

Plays performed in Dayton, Ohio were on Broadway or in Los Angeles last year, so your educational process should include an overview of what's happening in the major production centers.

University Study

The quality of an actor's education ebbs and flows relative to a faculty's ability to produce students that work in the business, so if you have the financial resources to attend the school of your dreams, I urge you to do extensive research before making your final decision.

There is a wealth of information available if you sharpen your investigative tools. When someone recommended Rutgers University, I checked their webpage and found that the chairman of the graduate department is the highly regarded William Esper. Esper lists the names of successful actors he has trained.

Your information gathering should include evaluating the background of the faculty, checking the curriculum and making sure there is a full time program for actors that includes training in speech, voice and movement.

One of the reasons that top schools are able to produce successful actors is that they will routinely see 600 women and 400 men in searching for the 8 women and 12 men they will admit. Their student body has already been screened to include only the creme de la creme.

Although requirements for admission into conservatory programs are rigorous, they are usually based solely on one's audition.

Some actors, writers and directors who attended these highly touted schools tell me they don't feel their education is necessarily superior, but that the network of achievers they encountered was worth the tuition.

Preferred Schools

There is a list of schools whose graduates in the acting program instantly alert the antennae of agents, producers and casting directors. These actors are perceived as the next Paul Newman and Meryl Streep. If nothing else, the buyers realize that the actors were so rigorously pre-screened in addition to the demanding course of studies that the chances of their having the potential for stardom is enhanced.

The list of schools whose graduates are anointed for brilliance varies slightly depending on whom you interview. No one wants to take responsibility for saying one school belongs and another one doesn't.

So based on hearsay and research, these are at least thought of by more people than others, to be *the* schools for actors at this moment in time.

All the schools have webpages, so if you are computer literate, check them out for an overview of the school and its curriculum. Some of the webpages are more user friendly than others, so be patient.

American Conservatory Theater/Carey Perloff
30 Grant Ave.
San Francisco, CA 94108
415-834-3200
Website: http://www.act-sfbay.org/conservatory/index.html

Carnegie Mellon/Drama Department/Peter Frisch
College of Fine Arts/School of Drama/Room #108
5000 Forbes Ave.
Pittsburgh, PA 15213
412-268-2392
Website: http://www.cmu.edu/cfa/drama/

Juilliard School/Kathy Hood, Director of Admissions
60 Lincoln Center Plaza
New York, NY 10023
212-799-5000 Extension 4
Website: http://www.collegeedge.com/details/college/1/58/d4_658.asp

New York University/Drama Department
Arthur Bartow, Artistic Director
721 Broadway, 3rd Floor
New York, NY 10003
212-998-1850
Website: http://www.nyu.edu/tisch/

North Carolina School of the Arts/Gerald Freedman
PO Box 12189/1533 Main St.
Winston-Salem, NC 27117-2189
336-770-3235
Website: http://www.ncarts.edu/

Northwestern University School of Speech/Dean David Zarefsky
1905 Sheridan Rd.
Evanston, IL 60208-2260
847-491-3741.
Website: http://www.rtvf.nwu.edu

State University of New York (at Purchase)/Israel Hicks
735 Anderson Hill Rd.
Purchase, NY 10577
914-251-6830
Website: http://www.purchase.edu/academic/taf/index.htm

University of California, Irvine
Admissions & Relations,
204 Administration Bldg.
Irvine, CA 92697-1075
949-824-6703
Website: http://www.arts.uci.edu/drama/

University of Missouri @ Kansas City
UMKC Theater Department/Cal Pritner, Chairman
404 Performing Arts Center/4949 Cherry Rd.
Kansas City, MO 64110
816-235-2702
Website: http://cei.haag.umkc.edu/theater/index.html

The State University of New Jersey/Rutgers
Mason Gross School of the Arts
William Esper, Director of Graduate Program in Acting
Rutgers Office of Graduate and Professional Admissions
Van Nest Hall, PO Box 5053
New Brunswick, NJ 08903-5053
908- 932-7711
Website: http://mgsa.rutgers.edu/mgsa/academics/grad4.html

University of Washington/School of Drama
Steven Pearson, Professional Student Program
PO Box 353950
Seattle WA, 98195-3950
206-543-0714
Website: http://artsci.washington.edu/drama/index.html

Yale Drama School/Yale University/Stan Wojewodski
PO Box 208325,
New Haven, CT 06520-8325
203-432-1505
Website: http://www.yale.edu/drama/

The Yale Drama School webpage offers
information on a variety of theater related schools and

subjects. They offer links to the schools above plus more at http://www.yale.edu/drama/links/resources.html

Options

If you want to be an actor in order to play Macbeth or Lady Macbeth, perhaps you can do that in your own hometown. Local theater productions can be very rewarding. You might play bigger parts with more regularity than you ever would as a professional actor. If you are really serious about acting all the great parts, perhaps you will become a repertory actor. There are interesting rep groups all over the country.

In Costa Mesa, a seaside community southeast of Los Angeles, there is a core group of actors who have worked together since producers Martin Benson and David Emmes created South Coast Repertory (SCR) over 25 years ago. These actors have played hundreds of parts. They don't make huge salaries, but they make a decent wage, are highly thought of within their community and they make their living doing what they love. They certainly embody the term *working actor*. SCR received a Tony in 1988 for contribution to theater in general, and to playwrights in particular.

For a quarter, Actors Equity Association will send you lists of theaters across the country which include the specific categories of dinner theater, Broadway, small theater, etc. There are currently six lists available for $1.50 plus a self-addressed-stamped envelope.

Actors Equity 5757 Wilshire Blvd. Hollywood, CA 90036 323-462-2334	Actors Equity 165 W 46th St. New York, NY 10036 212-869-8530

When I logged onto Equity's website at

http://www.actorsequity.org/, I found information about artists' grants from Theater Communications Group (TCG), general actor news, and specific casting news for all across the country. They also listed audition hotlines for four cities. For those of you without internet access, here are the numbers: New York; 212- 869-1242; Chicago; 312-641-0418; Los Angeles; 323-634-1776 and San Francisco 415-434-8007.

Entertainment Auditioning Centers

There are several theater conferences around the country that hold annual auditions for actors.

Straw Hat provides a place for non-Equity actors to audition for 30 theaters on the East Coast and 15 on the West Coast in February and March. It costs $30 to participate in one or $40 for both. You can get on the list in the Fall. When you write, be sure to include a stamped, self-addressed #10 envelope. You don't have to send money until you are accepted.

Straw Hat
Box 1187
Port Chester, NY 10573

The New England Theater Conference is another invaluable resource. Fifty-six Equity and non-Equity theaters attend their March auditions. NETC routinely receives 1,200-1,500 applications and chooses 500. The cost of membership is $25. Auditioning fees are extra, but even so, an affiliation with this group is worth the money. The NETC provides too much information and opportunity for employment to list here. My advice is to become a member and get their newsletter. NETC has opportunities and information for actors and technicians on every level.

New England Theater Conference (NETC)
c/o Theater Department
North Eastern University
Boston, MA 02115
617-373-2244

Other programs that screen talent for professional theaters are:

East Coast Theater Conference
Montclair State College
Montclair, NJ 07042
201-655-5112

The Southeastern Theater Conference (SETC)
Greensboro, NC 27420
910-272-3645

Staying Home

There may be many opportunities for work in your own community that have not occurred to you. If you intend to enter the national marketplace, the best thing you can do is spend a number of years in your own city exploiting and developing all of your talents.

Many of the Los Angeles job opportunities that I mention have some counterpart in your home town. Working with creative people anyplace will move you along your path, whether it is at a university, a museum or your local radio or television station. Get involved any way you can.

When I worked at the Cherry County Playhouse in Traverse City, Michigan, our cast visited a restaurant that had three shows nightly featuring singing, dancing and skits. This work was grueling, demanding and didn't pay a lot, but the young entertainers who were fortunate enough to get these summer jobs, were, in essence, being paid to go to graduate school. These students all found their opportunities though notices at their local colleges.

Worthy, Livable Goals

Acting is but a small piece of the pie. You will have a greater chance of success and have a more rewarding career if you can have the vision to embrace all areas of the business.

While I was researching the book I wrote for directors, *Directing Your Directing Career*, I happily discovered Roger Corman's book, *How I Made a 100 Films in Hollywood and Never Lost a Dime*. That book made me want to be starting my career all over again.

It's always hard to break into a closed system, whether it is show business or IBM, but if you allow yourself to go through any door that is open, instead of waiting for *the one*, your chances for success are greatly enhanced. Not only are you likely to find work sooner, but you may find a better niche that would have never occurred to you.

In a small marketplace, it is easier to become the writer, director and/or producer of whatever is going on. The steps it takes to bring a creative idea to fruition are the same where you live as they are in New York or Los Angeles.

Hard as it might be to believe, acting is looked upon as the lowest rung of the creative ladder by the rest of the creative community.

When I lived in Dallas as a young woman, it was easier to make money as a director than as an actor, so I directed. I also wrote and produced. At that point my mind was totally open; I was pretty clear about the fact that I didn't know a lot, so I asked anyone I could corner for advice and help. I just wanted to be engaged in theater, film or television.

It didn't occur to me to want to play Lady Macbeth, all I really knew was that being an actor seemed like a way to escape my life. Anything that smacked of show business looked like a movie to me and I wanted to do it.

I remember my first day of acting class in college;

the venerable Myrtle Hardy telling us that we should take any opportunity to get up in front of people. What a gift she gave me. Until that time, I had thought people would think I was *pushy* or *stuck on myself* or *conceited* (they would have, it was high school, after all), but now I had been told, that as part of my training, I should take every chance to get up in front of people and perform. I can still remember the sense of freedom I felt.

People probably did think I was stupid, pushy, crazy or worse. It didn't matter for I was on a mission. From where I am sitting now, I can only wish that my aspirations had been higher. Although I was willing to do whatever it took, my mind was clearly set on acting. Today, I realize that actors with truly great careers did not just act.

◆   *For all her well-known setbacks in the 1930s, including her disastrous 1933 Broadway appearance in* The Lake *(which inspired Dorothy Parker's famous putdown that she "ran the gamut of emotions from A to B") Katharine Hepburn never had trouble making her own opportunities. She had the wherewithal to tie up the film rights to* The Philadelphia Story, *the Broadway vehicle that she knew she could ride to a Hollywood comeback.*
A Wild Desire to Be Absolutely Fascinating
Frank Rich
The New York Times Book Review
September 29, 1991

So open your brain. Let your goal be to be successful in showbusiness — wherever that takes you. Some of the best directors I have ever worked with were once actors and they would never trade in the power and vision they command as directors for the mere visibility of being an actor. Many writers and producers from acting backgrounds feel the same way.

What Can I Do At Home?

There are advantages to staying home:

- You get to stay with the people you love
- You live in a familiar environment
- Unless you already live in NY, LA or San Francisco, it will undoubtedly be cheaper
- You already have a support group

Just because you are going to stay home (wherever that is) doesn't mean you can't keep abreast of what is happening in the large entertainment centers. As a young actor/director/writer in Texas, I made it a point to see every New York touring production that came to town. I was able to absorb lighting and staging ideas I would never have thought of on my own.

Besides staying up to date on the business, it's important to assess what jobs are available and how you can fit into the existing scheme of things.

When I was in high school trying to figure out how one goes from studying acting and being in local plays to making the jump into the big time, I decided to write my MGM musical idols for advice. Among the three people I wrote (who *all* answered me) were the late Gower Champion and his wife, Marge, star dancers for MGM at that time who both went on to choreograph and direct on Broadway.

Ms. Champion wrote me a wonderfully warm and detailed letter telling me that the best thing to do was to stay in Dallas until I had done everything there was to do in my hometown and then go to New York and study at The Neighborhood Playhouse or with Herbert Berghof at The HB Studios. Even though I didn't get to New York until 15 years later, I still followed her excellent advice.

Unless you are dropdead beautiful and your beauty is dying on the vine, there is every reason for you to refine your craft in a more protected environment. Then you can enter the bigger marketplace with training, credits and hopefully, a savings account.

Although you may not be able to make a living as an actor on the stage in your home town (that's pretty hard to do even in Los Angeles and New York), there are many variations on that theme that offer a chance to make money.

Book Reviews

Most people think of book reviews as being something you read, but there are actors who make a nice living by reading a current best seller, compiling a sort of verbal *Cliff's Notes* and presenting it for various service organizations as entertainment. I always wanted to do a book review with a stack of 8x10s of famous actors and cast the parts as I tell the story; *This part should be played by Elizabeth Taylor* (and hold up her picture) and so on. They would immediately know just what you are talking about. Have a 10, a 15, and a 20 minute version prepared and tailor the material to the needs of the audience.

Local Radio & Television

Call your local stations and ask what the possibilities are for employment on the air. If there is no one to talk to there, look in the Yellow Pages under advertising agencies and call them. Ask who hires on-camera or radio talent, note the name and ask to speak to him. Say something like: *Hi, I'm Mary Smith. I'm an actress and I'm interested in finding out who hires actors for commercials.*

When you get that person on the phone, reintroduce yourself and say that you would like to come by and meet him. If you have a picture and resume, mention that. If you have done any jobs that might impress, mention those.

When you call, do so late in the day. Frequently the secretary is gone and your future employer will pick up his own phone. Be up, personable, brief, energetic and specific. Arrange a meeting. Go. Be on time. Be professional and be strong. Don't play *like-me-like-me*, but do indicate that you are willing to learn and are a hard worker. Show that by arriving a few minutes early. Get your bearings in the hall before you enter the office. Just take time to collect yourself. Make sure you have read the morning newspaper so that you can have something interesting to talk about other than yourself.

If that person can't help you, ask him for advice on who else to speak to or what to do next. People love to give advice.

Cable Television

In every marketplace, there are locally produced cable television shows. You can actually produce your own. You don't even need a camera. In Los Angeles, there is a bargain shopper on a major local news show whose career started when she produced her own weekly cable access show. Today, she also writes a weekly news column in *The Los Angeles Times*. A young comic I know produced a funny restaurant guide show that is now part of CBS nightly local Los Angeles news.

Teach or Start Your Own Theater

It's not that difficult to get a job teaching acting at a local school or at the YMCA/YWCA. Decide whether you want to teach children, teenagers or adults, or all of the above. You can put notices up in your local supermarket, church, or post office announcing your classes.

Teaching is not only a means of making money and feeling fulfilled, but it also focuses one's thinking and makes one a better actor. Degreed credentials are helpful, though by no means essential. We all have encountered teachers without heart, empathy, insight and passion who had very impressive degrees, but were not inspiring in any way. Great teachers (and great directors) arouse the actor's passion and motivate him to resonate in ways he never thought of. If you feel you don't know how to teach, pattern your work on the best acting teacher you ever had and read books by great teachers (Allan Miller's book, *A Passion for Acting* or Uta Hagen's book *Respect for*

Acting) for inspiration. I also really love Michael Shurtleff's book *Audition* for acting insight whether as an actor or as a teacher.

Whatever your format, find a way to present your students before the public. Write or find plays that have to do with the holiday of the moment and produce something short. It's more fun to study acting when you know you'll have a place to show off your new abilities.

Or start your own theater and teach acting on the side. That way your students can have the possibility of auditioning for your own productions. Choose a play you love that has a small cast and one set. It's not that hard.

Other Jobs

Survival Jobs for Artists: Being Creative is Great...But So Is Eating written by enterprising actor Deborah Hershey is a good place to check out job ideas no matter where you live. It is published by Broadway Press.

Wrap Up

✓ check your hometown advantages and options
✓ evaluate the big marketplaces
✓ study your craft
✓ choose worthy livable goals
✓ be open to all opportunities

4　Why Do You Want To Be An Actor?

Life is very short. I tell my kids this all the time. Youth is over in about 15 minutes. Therefore it is important not to squander what our society prizes as the most energetic, attractive part of life by chasing a rainbow whose pot of gold may not be what you want.

Just because acting seems to appeal to others doesn't mean it would appeal to you. I sometimes think the unavailability of the jobs is the thing that appeals to actors the most. Maybe if everybody chose me, I wouldn't even be interested. So far, my win/loss ratio has kept that from being a problem.

What is it about acting that appeals to you? Are you truly interested in the process of creating a character? Does being a psychological sleuth attract you? Do you have a need to communicate? Are you an exhibitionist? Are your feelings about acting based on any realistic appraisal of what an actor's life is all about?

I was raised on a diet of movie musicals, and as a five-year old, could easily tell that Betty Grable and Esther Williams seemed to be living a much more exciting life than any grownups I ever saw. In Dallas, no handsome men were bringing bouquets of long stemmed red roses to anybody I knew. I had the idea that being an actress was something like *The Dolly Sisters*, or any one of a number of those old 20th Century Fox movies depicting life backstage.

After twenty years in the business, I must tell you, that for me at least, life as an actress has not been like a Betty Grable musical. Men have brought me long-stemmed red roses, but it had little to do with my being an actress. Well, maybe a little.

But the point is, I never saw Betty or Esther running around town picking up scripts, having to create an appropriate emotional climate for themselves to work in, auditioning for a room full of executives who had already seen ten other actresses who looked just like them. I never saw them rush from one appointment to another, changing hairdos and clothes at red lights, dealing with parking or subways and surly secretaries while trying to stay centered and concentrated on audition material. I'm not knocking this. I'm tickled to have an audition to go to. I just didn't have the faintest notion that acting involved these things.

I never saw Betty or Esther take an acting class or work with the flu or worry about a sick child. But then, they never had children in those stories either. Just roses. They never passed through age categories that put them out of work for years. It seemed they changed from young and adorable to middle-aged and responsible and then grandparent material in a cinematically authentic manner, without a hitch.

Of course, in real life, neither of those ladies had a life long career; Betty phased out when she got a little older and Marilyn came in and Esther quit the business when she married.

Before You Study Acting, Study the Lifestyle

In order to make an intelligent decision about acting as a way to spend your life, do the research. It's a shame the only biographies of actors that we are exposed to are those who have been successful. It would be more instructive to talk to actors who never made a dime in the business. Because the public is usually exposed only to star actors' lives, the idea of an actor's life is pretty much like what we see in the movies.

I have a friend who is a television editor. He has worked in the business all his life. Even so, he had never had an actor for a friend before we met. He was dumbfounded to find out all actors did not make the salaries reported in the newspapers. Nobody really wants to read that although an actor's minimum pay for a day on film is $576, he may not work more than two days per year, if that.

Acting is a profession. Any profession requires a big commitment. Years of study. Years of struggle. If your family is very wealthy, that may not be such a sacrifice, but the real challenge is not just doing without money, it's doing without validation.

When your life is spent with people saying, *No, thank you*, all the time, it takes effort to stay positive. Psychologists tell us that we get our picture of ourselves from our work. If you are not working, it's difficult to get a valid sense of self.

The reality is that every actor spends more time unemployed than employed and that his real job is looking for work. Stardom is after all, only unemployment at a higher rate of pay.

The actor's life is grueling. For a long time, you may not be able to have a life other than pursuing work and when you finally do get work, you will work and pursue your next job at the same time.

Choice of career is not just the choice of one's nine-to-five endeavor, but the choice of lifestyle. Within the instability of the actor's life, it is difficult to plan for children, vacations, illness and other of life's other necessities, luxuries or surprises.

When you are unemployed, it's difficult not to be depressed and when you are working, there's little time for a mate and family.

So when you're available, you're depressed and when you're happy, you're unavailable. That can make an actor an undesirable mate. On the other hand, if you can remain balanced and remember that your mate and your kids are the ones who will be there for you when management won't, you can enjoy the luxury of time that periods of not working give you to be there when your kids get home from school, help them with their homework and be there on a day-to-day basis for your mate. Then when you do work, your family will be able to enjoy your good fortune, confident that you will not go to work and forget to come home. They will know family life is the first priority.

Communication

So far, we haven't even dealt with the word communication. Most actors might not cite the need to communicate as their initial reason for getting into acting. Whether or not it is your goal, there is no way you can play a role and not communicate your take on the character.

It's easy to acknowledge the influence that writers can have on the public, but we tend to think of actors as merely delivering the writer's message, but the persona of the actor determines the message.

Roseanne was a stand-up comedienne who wrote her own material when she created the character that has made her famous. That creation came out of what she felt about being a working class wife and mother. If she had written this material and someone else had played it, let's say Sally Field (who also plays working class women), wouldn't Sally, just by being Sally, have made the material completely different?

And if the producer had chosen Sally for the role of Roseanne, he would have been choosing Sally's trademark vulnerability instead of Roseanne's edge. Casting directors and producers can alter the material dramatically by their choice of actor.

You communicate by walking into a room, by the way you carry yourself, the clothes you wear and the time you take before you begin to speak.

If you have on an Armani suit, people will not only get the idea that you have money, but that style and trend are very important to you. If you never comb your hair nor take a bath, you're definitely giving an antisocial message.

It's not just our clothes, of course, it's our mannerisms and tone of voice and body language that communicate who we are.

I remember a conversation I had years ago with a friend of my daughter's. As a student at UCLA, she was appalled that another student had spit on her as she was sitting on campus. I agreed with her that just because her normal attire was green hair, clown white makeup and strange clothes, that did not give anyone the right to spit at her. I did point out to her, however, that it was not the sort of apparel that advertised her sociability.

If you were lost and penniless on the subway platform, who would you ask for help? I would approach the most friendly looking person there.

Check the message your packaging is sending and make sure you are expressing your true voice. One of the problems with being trendy is that the meaning is generally: *I don't really have a message here, so I'm latching onto someone else's.*

Communicating at Auditions

If you create a character and attend an audition in that guise, you are making a statement about how you see that character played. It may or may not be the idea the director has, but you will have at least impressed him as someone who has a point of view and is not afraid to take responsibility for it.

Whether you are the good one, the bad one, the weird one, the banker or the killer, the more identifiable you are as a something, the easier it will be for casting people to plug you into the system. The bad news, of course, is that you will feel type cast. We should all be so lucky. Worry about that after you are employed.

Billy Bob Thornton's quirky character in *Slingblade* is not the only person he can play, but if you've seen other performances by this talented actor/writer, you will probably agree that you could not get another actor to play weird vulnerability more successfully. Gwyneth Paltrow's lovely sensibility was finally showcased perfectly in *Shakespeare in Love*. The vulnerable upper class young woman seeking adventure is her most winning role. John Malkovich's most effective characters are people we would not like to meet on a dark street.

Sally Kirkland (who is extremely career oriented)

won an Academy Award nomination in *Anna* for playing an actress who will do anything to get a job.

The biggest break I ever had as an actress was my first film. In *Joe*, I played the wife of a working-class man; a woman who was raised to say yes and keep her man happy. I had been in training for years as a Catholic wife and mother. I don't think I was that great an actress necessarily, it's just that who I was turned out to be perfect for the part. It was one of those rare synergistic miracles.

Meryl Streep is a good example of someone who has played a wide variety of parts. She's the queen of characterization using different accents and wigs, body behavior and varied social class. The one thing that is common in her work is her intelligence. You have never seen Ms. Streep play someone who is dumb.

Diane Sawyer is another persona that you look at and say smart; Jane Fonda, strong; Kevin Costner, all-American honesty; Jack Nicholson, devilishly dangerous and on and on. If you catch any of these performers on television in reruns of their early work, you will see the essence even then; time and experience have only honed that quality to its most commercial aspects.

What Makes You So Special?

Let's focus on what about you is special. What do you want to say? You can't be someone who says, *I don't know*, when you are asked which restaurant you want to go to. You can't say, *I don't care*, when someone asks where you want to sit in the theater.

Have an opinion and know what you want. People should be able to answer a lot of questions just by looking at you. If you don't know the answer, you can't communicate it. They don't pay the big bucks for averageness, unless you are so average you can be the prototype, as Ron Howard was in *Happy Days*. The people who will work in the business are those who can communicate a particular essence in the dramatic sense.

In Sidney Lumet's illuminating book, *Making Movies*, he speaks of the importance of self-knowledge.

✦   *In* Murder on the Orient Express, *I wanted Ingrid Bergman to play the Russian Princess Dragomiroff. She wanted to play the retarded Swedish maid. I wanted Ingrid Bergman. I let her play the maid. She won an Academy Award.*

I bring this up because self-knowledge is important in so many ways to an actor. Earlier, I mentioned how improvisation can be an effective tool in rehearsal as a way of finding out what you're really like when, for example, you're angry.

Knowing your feelings lets you know when those feelings are real as opposed to when you're simulating them. No matter how insecure, almost all the stars I've worked with have a high degree of self-knowledge. They may hate what they see, but they do see themselves. I think it's self-knowledge that serves as the integrating element between the actor's natural persona and the character he's playing.

> *Making Movies*
> Sidney Lumet
> Alfred A. Knopf
> New York 1995

Elizabeth Dillon at HB Studios in New York, was one of the best teachers for beginning actors in the business. Her ability to be clear about acting choices set her apart from all other teachers I have experienced. Dillon said *drama is heightened reality.* Not just a sigh, but the most profound sigh. Not just a tear, but the most poignant tear. Not just a laugh, but a contagious laugh.

New York agent, Michael Kingman, a whirlwind personality on his own, spoke of his ideal client: an actor with *contagious emotions.*

Look in the dictionary. It says that dramatic is *vivid, startling, highly effective, striking.* Are you? It takes a lot of energy to be fascinating and it's no accident.

You better not be just pretty. You better be beautiful. Pretty is a dime a dozen in the marketplace. You can even be ugly and have a career, but you better be *really* ugly. Phyllis Diller is an attractive woman, yet she made a career making us think of her as horse-faced. Whether you are extremely fat or extremely thin, you'd better have or create a look for yourself that is unique and then develop a persona to match it.

Ricki Lake is a brilliant example of this kind of thinking:

✦ *For the record, though she's sick of talking about it, Lake lost over 100 pounds between* Hairspray *and the premiere of her talk show. "My being fat was a gimmick and now my being like a normal person is a gimmick. It was definitely calculated. I looked at this business and decided you have to stand out in some way to get work. It'll be nice when people don't care anymore."*
Ricki's Gimmick
Joshua Mooney
Movieline
April 1994

Ricki's business acumen is astonishing in one so young. It helped that John Waters was a friend and fan, but either way, she definitely found a way to distinguish herself.

French Stewart, who stars in the popular comedy, *Third Rock from the Sun* experienced more success when he changed his perspective and his appearance:

✦ *Finally, after appearing in more than fifty plays in the Los Angeles area, Stewart started to look at his career as a business — in addition to being an art — and at himself as a product. "After several years of struggling, I felt I should have been doing better. I mean, I was working a lot, but I don't think I was necessarily working smart."*
It was a sobering moment for the actor. "I had to figure

out, 'How was I going to market myself? What can I do best?'"
The answer came to him quickly: 'be weird.' The first thing he did
was shave his head.

"I got myself this blue jacket that looks like a utility
jacket," he says. "I even have real scars on my head, so when I
shaved it, I really looked weird. The combination of those two things
knocked the retardation look right over the wall."

It was that change in persona that got him noticed. He
started getting bit parts on shows like Seinfeld and The Larry
Sanders Show. "Shaving my head sort of got my foot in the
door," he says.

Rock 'n Roll
Kathleen O'Steen
Emmy
August 1997

Terry and Bonnie Turner, the husband and wife
team who were searching for cast members for Third
Rock said, *although French did stand out because of his odd look,*
that they had seem lots of odd looking guys, *it was his
ability to deliver, that clinched the deal:*

✦   *He was just really really funny and he was warm and
wonderful.*

Rock 'n Roll
Kathleen O'Steen
Emmy
August 1997

Confidence, Determination & Drive

Talent, looks and youth are all good, but nothing
succeeds like confidence, determination and drive.

The ability to feel within yourself that you can do
anything (even if you can't) will take you far. You have to
set fear aside and go for it. Will Smith is a stunning
example of just doing it.

Will's father is a military man who built his own
refrigeration business. One summer he remodeled his ice

house, tore down its old brick wall and told Will and his
brother that they were to build a new one:

✦　　*I couldn't believe it. He wanted us to build a wall 50 feet
long and 14 feet high. I remember standing there and thinking,
"There's no way I will live to see this completed. He wants us to
build the Great Wall of Philly!"*
　　*I remember hoping my father would get committed, because
if he were in an insane asylum, then we wouldn't have to finish the
thing. But finally we did. And I remember my father standing there
looking at us, and all he said was, "Now don't ever tell me there's
anything you can't do."*
　　*He'd been waiting six months just to deliver that line.
And I got it: there's nothing insurmountable if you just keep laying
the bricks, you know? You go one brick at a time and eventually
there* <u>*will*</u> *be a wall.*
　　*You can't avoid it. So I don't worry much about walls. I
just concentrate on the bricks, and the walls take care of themselves.*
　　Iron Will
　　Joe Rhodes
　　Premiere
　　November 1998

Will was a successful rapper mugging in music
videos when Quincy Jones managed to sell a network on
the idea of Smith starring in his own sitcom. A week
before shooting, Smith began to get nervous:

✦　　*This is ridiculous. Is anyone ever going to ask me whether
or not I can act? So, I'm sitting at home, flipping though channels,
and there are all these shows — sitcoms, movies, soap operas —
and all these actors, thousands and thousands of actors. And that's
when it hits me, I said to myself, "it's not mathematically possible
that all these people are better than me. Nature doesn't allow that.
At worst, I have to be better than half of them, right?" And this
weird comfort washed over me. I knew I'd be okay.*
　　Iron Will
　　Joe Rhodes
　　Premiere
　　November 1998

People who know Smith say he has the best disposition in the world and along with that, he works harder than most people, but he will tell you that his greatest asset is his drive:

◆   *...I see people all the time who are better rappers than me, better actors than me, better-looking and stronger than me. But my ace in the hole is my dangerously obsessive drive, you know? I'm a terminator. I absolutely, positively will not stop until I win.*
        Iron Will
        Joe Rhodes
        Premiere
        November 1998

If you canvas Smith's body of work, you will see that his drive and good nature are featured prominently in his characters. He seems to be able to know who he is and use it.

Being who you really are sounds easy, however most actors have spent a lifetime trying to become what they thought would please others or at the other extreme, behaving badly, just for effect. The process of owning one's real feelings comes in fits and starts.

Do you prefer red or blue? Corduroy or velvet? Rice Krispies or yogurt? How do you feel about gay people? Politics? Violence? What's your favorite music? Do you like candy? Do you eat meat? Are you formal? Casual? Flamboyant? Private? Do you even take the time to listen and find out the answers? Perhaps one of the answers is not to do so much: to listen more, to yourself as well as others.

Only when you have some of these answers will you project the energy necessary to communicate an essence. You will play many parts but, it's your defined presence that makes the statement interesting — or not.

I'm spending a lot of time talking about philosophy. That's appropriate since life is a mind-set. If you can conceptualize your goals accurately and specifically, you can plan a time table and select a role model. The more precise your mind-set, the more efficient your efforts and the more fruitful your results.

Wrap Up

You need to know the answers to these questions

- ✓ why do I want to act?
- ✓ do I really want the lifestyle?
- ✓ what do I want to say?
- ✓ what makes me special?
- ✓ do I believe I can do anything?
- ✓ do I have the drive and determination?

5   When? How?

The dictionary says an actor is: a person who acts in stage plays, motion pictures, television broadcasts, etc., especially professionally.

With that definition in mind, I have been an actor since I was five years old. That was when I was in my first play. The dictionary didn't say anything about tap dancing on Mona Ann Chadwick's front porch. We were too embarrassed to have them see us, so we stopped when the bus went by, so I'm not sure that counted, but I think that was acting, too. We are frequently destined to become actors well before we consciously make the commitment to making our living as performers.

Whenever civilians (people who are not in the business) come up to ask me questions about being an actress, they never ask a single question about how to act. Oh, some want to know how an actor *remembers all those lines*, but they all seem to think that, of course, they would be able to act. They easily conceptualize the process of enrolling in an acting school, but the thing that totally eludes them is how one translates acting ability into gainful employment. That concept also eludes many trained actors.

There is no big mystery. Translating dreams into reality simply entails being businesslike, focusing on the goal and marching toward it. Some people possess these skills naturally and others have to learn them. Some need to refine those skills, others just need support.

Write Your Life Story

Get a pencil and an important book to write in; a scrap of paper is not enough; you are going into business, so make sure your plans are stored appropriately. You will be referring to your notebook/journal frequently, so make sure it is user friendly and reflects your style. Also you want it to bring a good price after you are famous and they auction it off.

Resist the temptation to use your computer or typewriter. There is a potent visceral force unleashed by the act of forming the words with your hands that takes thought one step closer to reality.

Write down all your best fantasies. They don't have to be realistic, but make sure they are attainable. You're not going to look like Tom Cruise, be ten years younger or a foot taller no matter how hard you work. Stick to the realms of possibility and probability. Do you want to win an Oscar? Own a Rolls? Speak French? Write it down. Live in the best part of town? Marry the person of your choice? Live happily ever after? Have three kids? No kids? Think, dream. Write everything down. Edit later. Let yourself go.

Don't forget to write down what you are willing to do in return. Delay starting a family? Study? Be original? Unique? Find ways of doing things that no one has ever done before?

Goals

Do you want to be a classical actor? A film actor? An actor who does television? Soaps? Theater? Do you intend to pursue your craft in your own home town? Do you intend to go to Los Angeles or New York? Can you make a living as an actor in Rapid City, South Dakota? Can you make a living in show business in Wilmington, Delaware? Can you be happy with the options available in your own hometown?

If you live in a small town and your goal is to be a respected actor, your first goal might be to get a part in a play. If there is not a theater group, start one. If there is a theater group, join it. Get a part if you can. If not, stage manage, help build sets, be the property master, just become active and demonstrate your reliability and your creative powers in whatever job is available. Your time to act will come. You will figure out how to make it happen.

Whether or not we identify them as such, we set goals all the time anyway which I realized, recently, when I ran into an old college friend. He reminded me that our first assignment in our college Public Speaking class was to introduce ourselves in some way to make people remember which one you were. I was alternately thrilled and mortified to hear him report that I had said: *I'm K Callan. You should remember my name because someday I am going to be famous and you are going to want to come swim in my swimming pool.*

You know what? When I moved to New York to finally seek fame and fortune, the subsidized low-income housing I lived in had a swimming pool and so does my home in California. From my Texas viewpoint, a swimming pool equated success as an actor. Since I was so powerful, I sure wish I had said: *Remember my name, I'm going to be the world's greatest actor and I will win five Oscars!*

As you conceptualize your goals, be informed and be specific. Focus carefully on what you want. If you commit to your goals, you will reach them.

Immediate Goals

Your immediate goal needs to be intimately related to your marketplace. It's unlikely you'll be able to win an Oscar in Valentine, Nebraska. But you could probably have a career in local radio in Valentine.

Take the most important thing on your list. Let's say it is to win an Oscar. Put a date on it. Say ten years from now. Then work backwards. What are the steps that would have to be taken before you could realize that goal? Perhaps your timetable might look like the chart on the following page.

Make sure you leave a space to check off your goals as you achieve them. As you will notice, this is a five-year plan. Set your own dates. If you manage to achieve some of these goals faster, fine. Some will be slower, but this is a pretty realistic schedule. For every goal, focus on what you are willing to do to accomplish it: lose weight, learn to sing, get a second job, give up junk food, ask for what you want, etc.

	Jan-Mar	Apr-Jun	Jul-Sept	Oct-Dec
Year 1	take acting classes/voice	join theater company	get a part in a play/explore book reviews research ad agencies for commercials	get name in news-paper re: current project
Year 2	get a bigger part more press	do another play	more of the same	Equity card
Year 3	get local commercial	more local commercials	assemble an audition tape	explore stand-up
Year 4	move to LA or NY*/get a place to live/fix it up	get an industry related job	get involved with theater company get pictures made	get in a play research casting directors
Year 5	get a com-mercial get a commercial agent join SAG	get a part in a student or low budget film - add to audi-tion tape start meet-ing casting directors	get another film part - revamp tape begin search for an agent get your name in the paper or do a radio interview	get thea-trical agent continue your agenting efforts - seeing casting people, etc.

* The best time to move to Los Angeles is in August and the best time to move to New York is in the Spring.

Make a Detailed Plan

If you wanted to build a house, it would be pretty clear that you would have to ask and answer a few questions. How much money do you have to spend? What kind of house do you want? Victorian? Modern? Country? Which architect designs that type of house well? What type of building materials will you use?

What kind of bathtub do you want? In order to answer that question, you would have to go all over town looking at the bathtubs that were available. You would need to price them and check their availability, find out whether or not you have to order one or they have it in stock. All this just for a bathtub. Can you imagine the kind of detail involved in truly planning a career?

In order to set goals for yourself as an actor, you'll need to answer specific questions to formulate a plan for success. Write about the life you want to lead: where you want to live it and what kind of house you want to live in. Describe the clothes you want to wear and the food you want to eat. Whether you want a cook or want to cook for yourself and your friends in a big family kitchen. Do you live alone? Are you married? Are you always involved with your current co-star? What? It's your story. No one else will read it.

Identify the roles you want to play. Discuss how you want a typical day in your life to be and visualize these goals on an emotional level. That is what engages the brain, focuses it and puts the plan into action.

Call this document *My Future*. It should take at least two weeks to formulate. Remember, you are starting a business. Since you are investing your life in this pursuit, protect your investment by doing meticulous research and planning. The more you conceptualize acting as a business as well as an artistic venture, the more successful you can be. You will also be less likely to personalize the rejection.

Compose a short version detailing your current goals and what you are willing to do for them. Read your intentions every day — first thing in the morning and last thing at night. You will experience your thought process beginning to change.

I read that years before any kind of validation came their way, Sonny and Cher used to drive to Bel Air and sit in front of the gates of one of the swankiest, most theatrically historic houses in town. They decided they would live in that house one day. They did.

To give you support in focusing your goals, I recommend an effective motivational tape (and there are many), *Think and Grow Rich* by Napoleon Hill. Hill is the original *positive thinking/you can do it* guru. He was saying things in 1937 that Anthony Robbins has enlarged upon today.

Another inspiring book is *The Artist's Way* written by Julia Cameron. The book goes into great detail about not only about goalsetting, but about learning about who you are and what you really want.

Be Specific

Paul Linke, one of the stars of the hit series, *CHiPS* wrote a one man show about his own life called *Time Flies When You Are Alive*. In it, he told an ironic story about being specific. He said he used to pray to *get a part in a hit series and but for the omission of a single word: quality, he might have ended up on* Hill Street Blues *instead of* CHiPS.

I have my own specific story and it coincidentally involves an audition for *Hill Street Blues*. The scene had to do with a woman who was hysterical because her no good boyfriend had left her. I could not seem to find a way to motivate myself using that scenario. I could motivate myself substituting one of my kids for the love object. I reasoned, tears of rejection are tears of rejection. It worked, the scene went very well. Only one hitch. After my reading, the producer stopped me and said, *Could you do it again with a different thrust? That kind of seemed like one of your kids left you instead of your boyfriend.*

They got it. They actually got what was going on in my mind although the words were totally different. What a powerful weapon! You can have whatever you can imagine. Decide what you want. These decisions are not written in stone. You can change them. But the more detailed your life script, the less chance of error!!

Wouldn't it be interesting to know how Sonny and Cher got from sitting in front of the house to owning it? Do you suppose their first big goal was a hit record? Maybe the immediate goal was just to get to a place where they were hanging around with people in the business they could learn from. Perhaps their next goal was getting a paying job singing.

Targeting signposts that let you know you are moving along will give you courage and inspiration when you need it most. When all seems dark, you can whip out your list and notice that, in fact, you have already accomplished A, B and C, even though D is eluding you at the moment. It's nourishing to notice when you make progress and celebrate it.

Support Groups

Find another ambitious actor to join you in your quest. You can be a team. Try for a team of four and make a commitment to support each other. Meet twice a month to talk about your plans and announce your newest goal. Check each other to see that you are really staying on the track, making time tables and keeping on them. At each meeting, choose a new goal or take the last one further. There is something magic about saying your intention to another human being. The energy gets into the air and becomes concentrated and powerful.

Choose a role model. What actor/actress has the career and life you would like to have? You will have your very own one day, but today it will help you to have a concrete picture of your goal. Get a picture of your role model and put it where you will see it every day. If you have a hard time choosing a role model, this may be telling you something about your ambivalence about the business.

Go to the library. Ask the person at the reference desk for all the sources of material written about your role model. Find out how he/she started and studied. If there's a biography, read it.

It's a good idea to give yourself the task of reading one showbiz biography every week. It is fascinating to find out how other people solved some of the same problems you have or will be faced with. It will be somewhat like inviting all those people over to brainstorm with you.

There are other practical nuts and bolts things we will talk about in the next chapter. For now, you have chosen your role model and I hope you've started a support group.

You can do all these things even before you study. Set study deadlines. Research the possibilities of teachers. Get a part time job at a theater or a radio or television station and see what some phase of show business looks like up close.

Start at any point in your life. It may be five years before you can expect to realistically be looking for an actual part, but that's okay. Begin to conceptualize today.

Groundwork

In an actor support group that I belong to, an actor began lamenting pilot season. A pilot is the first show of a proposed television series. Getting a pilot, whether or not it is sold, can make an actor's year financially.

George was upset that he was not being sent on as many auditions as he felt he was due. He wondered what he could do to enhance his chances. The group concurred that the most important work toward getting a pilot comes 9 to 12 months prior to pilot season. Actors chosen for pilots are frequently those actors who have done other interesting (usually less lucrative) work all season that has gotten their agent and/or the casting director excited about submitting them for pilots.

You have to get the part before you can get the award. The most effective way to do this is to become an entrepreneur. If you're not going to do that, you must be very lucky. Many are. There's an old saying, *I'd rather be lucky than good.* Me, I would rather be lucky and good.

Good Luck

In order to have good luck, one must understand its concept. Yes, you can create your own luck. But even so, life really is like one big poker game. You are never going to get all winning hands and you won't get all losing hands either. The trick is to make the most of the wins while you minimize the losses. Learn to play poker well.

Burt Reynolds was one of the great box office draws for many years. After a career of many ups and downs, Mr. Reynolds is no longer hot. Is it age? Self-destructiveness? Or could it be that he is not as entrepreneurial as his contemporary, Clint Eastwood, who still reigns at the movie box office. Clint has produced and directed many of his films. Two even more successful entrepreneurs are Sylvester Stallone and Arnold Schwarzenegger.

Positive Thinking

One of my favorite show business stories involves Eastwood and Reynolds. Contract players for Universal, they were called in on the same day and told their contracts were not being renewed. Management said neither of them had a future. Reynolds, because he couldn't act, and Eastwood, because of his unusually large Adam's apple. As they were walking off together, lost in thoughts of failure, Reynolds turned to Eastwood and said: *Well, I can learn to act. What are you going to do?*

We create our own lives. Successful people invent themselves.

Albert Hague was a Tony winning composer before his success as an actor on the television show, *Fame.* Since he had spent years on the other side of the table watching actors make major audition mistakes, he used to run a very helpful class in auditioning for musicals.

I took that class early in my career. Although he had many valuable things to teach about auditioning and the business, the one quote that keeps coming back to me had nothing to do with career: *It takes a lot of creative energy to have an interesting life.*

The real focus needs to be on your life. It can have as much excitement as you are willing to create. With all the statistics and casualties and hard work, you still can be that actor who consistently works in the smallest or the largest marketplace.

Wrap Up

✓ make a specific plan
✓ set goals with date
✓ consider what you are willing to do for them
✓ make a commitment
✓ join or form a support group
✓ it takes creative energy to have an interesting life

6 Getting Organized

It can get confusing and lonely pursuing goals independently. It's hard to tell if you are making progress, since there are so many tasks to accomplish. It's easy to become overwhelmed, run in many directions at once and accomplish nothing.

Since you are the architect of your career, no matter what else happens, you may as well look upon your career as your pursuit of a Ph.D. Inherent in that degree is the ability to initiate your own game plan as well as conceive a unique idea that no one in your field has exploited before.

The saving grace of being a candidate for the Ph.D. is you get your own private major professor. A person who discusses goals with you, puts you on the right track and monitors your progress. Some major professors are better than others, but you are getting a special major professor with only one student. You will be your own major professor.

What a concept for an actor. Since we are in the habit of playing parts anyway, if we conceptualize a part of ourselves as the major professor, we can slip into character, become wise and perhaps even gain perspective.

Sometimes when I can't figure out what to wear or combine with something, I will just say, *What would Ralph Lauren do?* and somehow I make the right choice. Just like air-conditioning, I don't know why it works, it just does.

First Things First

When you finally arrive in New York, Los Angeles, Chicago or wherever else you have chosen to pursue your acting career, there are certain basics of life that must be attended to before you should try to get an agent or a job.

◆ *Get a job and a nice place to live. Truthfully, you would be amazed. People take years to take care of that problem. In New York, especially, it's so important to have a base. One of our clients said in an interview recently that acting wasn't her life. Her life was her life. Acting was what she did. She loved doing it and didn't want to do anything else. But it wasn't her life.*

Whenever people said they were having problems with their acting and what could they do to change it, her response was always, "change your life." That's something young actors don't want to believe, but I think it's very true.

So if I just arrived in New York, I wouldn't worry so much about acting until I solved the problem of where I was going to live, how I was going to make a living and how I was going to get by day to day because I don't think you can solve anything else first.

Tim Angle
Abrams Artists, Los Angeles

Surviving on your own without a 9 to 5 job demands great courage and discipline. Nothing demands your attention at a specific moment. You can sleep until noon if you choose. There's no place you have to be. In the abstract, this sounds like heaven. The reality can be depressing and paralyzing.

The structure of a regular job demands some sort of mental health. There are times set for arriving, eating and leaving. There are tasks to be performed, people to talk to, people to rebel against and someone to pay you. There's frequently some type of dress code. When you are self-employed or in the case of the actor, mostly unemployed, the situation can awaken latent insecurities. Don't wait until all those primal needs are screaming at you to create a life for yourself. Start now.

Work Corner

Establish a work center that includes your desk, a bright lamp, a rolodex, phone, answering machine, book shelves with room for a reference library, plus storage space for all your office supplies, pictures, resumes, manila envelopes, mailing labels, computer or typewriter and good stationery.

Don't use this space (even if it is just a corner of your kitchen or bedroom) for anything but work. That way your unconscious will subtly begin to shift into business/creative mode every time you sit at your desk. I have a favorite chair I have endowed as my *inspiration chair* and I sit in it every time I read a script and prepare for an audition. I fully expect to have great inspiration every time I sit there and it usually works for me in a way no other space in my house does.

Keep a clock and a pad and pencil for messages by the telephone. There should be a pencil and pad next to every telephone in your house. Never keep a business contact waiting on the phone while you search the house for pencil and paper.

Looking For Work

Looking for work is our main job as actors. It is stressful to be constantly rejected. Just as being continually exposed to a virus soon wears the system down, your spirit is vulnerable to attack if you haven't made provisions for rejuvenation by controlling all the things you can. The familiarity of routine softens the effects of never knowing when you will be making money again, so make a list of things you commit to do daily. Set aside a specific time for each of these activities and stick to it.

Familiarity Breeds Comfort

Schedule a time for awakening and going to bed. You don't have to be fanatical about it, but the more you adhere to a schedule, the more secure you will feel. We are all comforted by the familiar.

It will make a difference.

Schedule errands for one particular day of the week and put a time frame around them. These tasks have a way of eating up energy. No matter how onerous, they are a lot more fun than calling up some person who might end up saying no to whatever we are asking.

My son-in-law, Don says, *errands are those things we do when we're not doing what we are supposed to do.* I agree.

Spiritual and Physical Health

No matter what, exercise daily and eat nutritiously. If you begin each day with stretching and exercise, you can assist your body's own natural resistance to both physical and emotional illness while keeping your instrument fit and in tune. Get sufficient sleep. If you feel yourself beginning to get depressed, check to see if these basics are taken care of.

It is important to take time for a regular sit down meal. And even if you can't resist eating self-destructively, counter that behavior by detoxifying your system as much as possible with good food. The famous nutritionist, Dr. Henry Beiler contends that green vegetables (the darker green the better) detoxify the system.

Students at The American Conservatory Theater in San Francisco benefitted greatly when Los Angeles' famous nutritionist, Eileen Poole, visited regularly on a volunteer basis to advise them on appropriate eating habits. She was so inspirational that the students actually gave up sugar and caffeine. One of those students, actress Annabella Price, told me that her mental outlook as well as her physical abilities improved dramatically as a result of her diet.

We have already discussed forming a support group for acting goals. It's even more important to have a regular family experience to support your personal life. If you don't have a family nearby, form one with members of your acting class or your neighbors or the people from the Laundromat. The operative words here are *create a family for yourself.* I believe one of the great lures of being an actor is the families we create when we work.

In his book, *The Right Place at the Right Time,*

employment consultant Dr. Robert Wegmann states:

To help maintain perspective: Exercise regularly...and keep in close contact with friends whom you trust and with whom you can share your experiences.

Life is problem solving, and challenges are easier to meet with the support of loved ones. It helps to be involved regularly with a group of people who recognize this, offer mutual support and encourage shared feelings.

If you don't have loved ones in the area, the 12-step groups are invaluable (Alcoholics Anonymous, Overeaters Anonymous, Adult Children of Alcoholics, etc.) They boil down to free group therapy any day of the week.

When we join existing support groups, we are usually in a vulnerable state and we are ready to lay down all our defenses in the hopes of feeling better. I'm not against that in concept, but retain your own persona and way of speaking. Don't throw out the baby with the bath water.

Some people go to church. Others practice yoga, the martial arts, or garden. Choose whatever might get you in touch with your own vitality. You will be stronger, more vulnerable and a better actor. The added self-esteem will help put your career in perspective.

Time Out

There are all kinds of meditation. I don't care which kind you choose, but it is vital to take 10-20 minutes twice a day for yourself. To take stock. To be silent. No music. No eating. No drinking. No talking. Just be with yourself. Not just when you think about it, or if it happens, but establish a regularly scheduled time for you and yourself. Many people believe these are the moments that allow you to tune in to your own feelings and intuitions. If you don't take the time to do this for yourself, you are shortchanging yourself as a person and as an actor.

It's a challenge to carve out time for nurturing

yourself. What motivates me is the possibility of getting work. If that time twice a day spent by myself, allows or encourages me to visualize my goals or to be quiet long enough to develop whatever it is that is going to separate me from the pack, I find a way to do it. I hope you will, too.

Class/Study/Teachers/Gurus

When I lived in New York, I went to dance classes Mondays, Wednesdays and Fridays, had a voice lesson on Tuesday morning and worked with an accompanist on Thursdays. I also went to acting class on Tuesday nights. Depending on your goals, you should be involved in some version of this. Classes not only improve our skills, but they keep us involved with people and plugged into the network of actors, and help structure our days.

A word here about teachers. I think most of us are looking for the secret of life, the answer or magic ingredient that is going to make life work better. I think actors believe in magic more than most people, so I caution you, if you can find a great teacher who can help you marshal your creative forces, whether you're in Podunk, New York or Hollywood, do it, but do not give up your own thought processes. Even very good and very reputable teachers sometimes have their own agenda. Perhaps it is religious or political or maybe their agenda is simply to get laid, but that's their path, not yours.

Since people are defined by their belief systems, don't allow anyone to trivialize yours. Refine them as you grow, but question, question, question. You don't have to be a pain in the butt about it and do it out loud, but a certain amount of skepticism is healthy. As an actor, all you have to sell is your *self*, so make sure it's still intact when class is over. Don't blindly follow anyone.

Acting is greatly entwined with our psychological well-being. That does not mean making our psyches vulnerable to just anyone who displays an interest. If you need help, get a reputable shrink and deal with your emotional problems there. Don't let acting teachers play in your mind.

If a teacher is opposed to anyone with other thought processes, watch out. If you stay with people who do not encourage you to question, how will you ever nurture your imagination and exercise your own creativity? Give yourself credit. A friend of mine left her acting class not long ago when the teacher declared: *You have really become a better actor since you began working with me.*

Maybe that was true. Also true was the fact that my friend didn't get a single job during the entire time she was in that class. I think the teacher just meant, *I like your acting better because you are getting to be so much like me.*

Get a Mentor

Many lucky people in show business have mentors. I think it's a rarity for actors in general, and women have an even tougher time finding another woman to mentor them; but I believe, man or woman, if your focus is on getting a mentor, you can.

A mentor differs from a role model in that role models are usually viewed from afar, whereas a mentor's work is to educate and lend a helping business hand to someone who is just beginning. They advise. They point out. They introduce.

How do you get one? As in most life situations, you have to ask. I'm not saying it will be easy, but if you choose someone in the business who you admire and think you could learn from and if you have a clear focused view of what you want from them, you can at least ask.

Find someone who has what you want and ask them questions. Readers frequently call me asking questions about agents. I always help them. My friends have warned:

You're going to be sorry. Everyone is going to take

advantage of you. They're wrong. It's mainly the winners who are smart enough to figure out how to call me. They don't whine and they are careful not to waste my time. They all have plans. And I (just like everyone else) love the opportunity to share what I know.

Mentors and role models can be quite helpful over the course of your life; but again, keep the skepticism meter handy. You don't want to become the mentor or role model, you just want to profit from their wisdom and encouragement. You can't have a mentor or a career if you are afraid to ask.

A Los Angeles organization called *Women in Film* has recently started a Mentor Program and I think it is the smartest thing they have done. Young women pick out someone, write a page about why they want this particular person to mentor them and *Women In Film* endeavors to work it out. Some wish list mentors don't have time and are not interested, but others remember how much they would have wanted help or want to repay help that was given them and sometimes it does work.

Perhaps there is some group in your town that would be interested in sponsoring a mentor program if the idea was pitched to them.

Focused Analytical Viewing

Study includes more than formal classes. Your education includes viewing other actors' work and analyzing what's good and what's lacking and why. There are ways of doing it though.

Focus on your goal. Greet every experience as though you were going to have to write a paper on it. It will keep you focused and in the present. Say to yourself before every meeting, even lunch with your friend, *What do I want from this experience? Lunch and to energize my friendship.*

If we all took the time to consciously think of such goals before our actions, we'd be less likely to get off the track, take a disagreement personally and get bogged down in negativity. If the goal is to make things work, not to be right, make points, or show someone the error of his ways, things do work and everyone has a better time. I took a class once with Stella Adler who used to strike terror in the hearts of students when she pointed at them and screamed: *Untalented!* Of course, we were all pretty happy when she pointed at us and beamed: *Talented.* It took me a little while to gain enough perspective to understand that what she was saying was: *That is an untalented choice. This is a talented choice.* We make choices everyday in the way we choose to view things.

Untalented Viewing Comments

- I hated that movie.
- That play was no good.
- That actor stinks.

Talented Viewing Comments

- The movie moved too slowly and was not focused.
- The play didn't work for me because the lead was miscast. It required someone more flamboyant.
- Gee, she's usually so good. It's good to remember that we can all be bad. I wonder what happened.

Begin to think in a problem solving way. Not only will you be more interesting to be around, since you will be looking for a solution, but you'll be sending out positive energy. It takes so much more effort to be positive than negative, but it pays off 100%. The bottom line is, of course, that you get smarter, but the by product is that you're a whole lot nicer to be around.

Your Laboratory

As part of your education as an actor, get a job

working in the business in some area other than acting. Be an usher in the theater or work in an agent's office or at a television station. Be a gopher. You will begin to get a clearer idea of the lifestyle. It may not be as appealing up close. If that is the case, think of all the time and heartache you have saved yourself.

When I was interviewing agents for *The New York Agent Book* I met a young woman who was assisting a famous agent. She was an aspiring actress who had come to New York from a small town. After spending two years seeing firsthand how it really is, she no longer wants to be an actress. She now perceives the rejection as too depressing and it no longer appeals to her. She now wants to be a producer and have power and a decent lifestyle.

Read Show Business Books

You should have your own library of showbiz reference books which list the credits of actors, writers, directors, producers and casting executives along with biographies that give you another peek into the actor's lifestyle. There have been some candid books in the recent past which delineated the real scoop on what goes on behind the scenes.

Here is a list of books that will give your library a good start:

The Actor's Audition/David Black
Adventures in the Screen Trade/William Goldman
AFTRA Agency Regulations
The Artist's Way/Julia Cameron
Audition/Michael Shurtleff
casting by ... A directory of the Casting Society of
    America, its members and their credits
*The Complete Directory to Primetime Network TV
    Shows*/ Tim Brooks-Earle Marsh
The Devil's Candy/Julie Salamon
Equity Agency Regulations

The Film Encyclopedia/Ephraim Katz
The Filmgoer's Companion/Leslie Halliwell
Final Cut/Steven Bach
Halliwell's Film Guide/Leslie Halliwell
*How I Made 100 Films in Hollywood and Never Lost a
      Dime*/Roger Corman
Hype & Glory/William Goldman
Indecent Exposure/David McClintock
The Los Angeles Agent Book/K Callan
Making Movies/Sidney Lumet
My Lives/Roseanne
The New York Agent Book/K Callan
New York Times Directory of Film/Arno Press
New York Times Directory of Theater/Arno Press
*Next: An Actor's Guide
      to Auditioning*/Ellie Kanner-Paul Bens
Reel Power/Mark Litwak
Ross Reports Television/Television Index
Saturday Night Live/Doug Hall-Jeff Weingrad
Screen Actors Guild Agency Regulations
Screen World/John Willis
The Season/William Goldman
Survival Jobs for Artists/Deborah Hershey
Theater World/John Willis
TV Movies/Leonard Maltin
Wake Me When It's Funny/Garry Marshall
*Who's Who in the Motion
      Picture Industry*/Rodman Gregg
Who's Who in American Film Now/James Monaco
Wired/Bob Woodward

If you know of any books that belong on this list,
let me know and I'll include them in future editions.

Books like *Wired, Indecent Exposure* and *Saturday
Night Live* detail the costs of becoming famous. Keeping
them on your bookshelf and reading them from time to
time will encourage you to keep your values in
perspective. It's easy to get caught up in the glamour,
publicity, money and power of this fairytale business.
These things can leave as quickly as they come. Success

won't fix you. You may feel better for a while, but you're always you — just with a different set of problems.

I cannot stress strongly enough the need for a good reference library.

For fun, read Tony Randall's book, *Which Reminds Me*; for inspiration, Carol Burnett's *One More Time*; and to hear about more bad luck than you'll ever have, read Charles Grodin's *It Would Be So Nice if You Weren't Here.* Roseanne's book, *My Lives,* speaks candidly of the behind the scenes intrigue involved with her show. It's instructive. Garry Marshall's book, *Wake Me When It's Funny* shares some great attention getting ideas for everybody in the business.

There are many other helpful books. These are just ideas for a starting library. Schedule time each day for business related reading. Whether this means browsing your local newspaper for audition announcements or noticing who just took over an ad agency or when the local Lion's Club might need a speaker, do it regularly.

Money Wisdom

There's no guarantee that a prestigious acting job will enable you to pay your rent. Off Broadway and chorus jobs don't pay much and decent showcases (for which there is great competition) don't pay anything at all. And sometimes a job paying a lot of money can end up being a trap. It's very seductive to work every day and make good money. If you are on a soap opera or a television series, you are lucky to be employed for several years, but you only get to play one role. Many actors in this position have yearned to leave those jobs for what they felt would be more artistically challenging work, but big money can make any artistic decision hard to make.

Other actors, who do not have as visible or lucrative careers, are frequently more fulfilled though much less regularly employed because they choose to have the opportunity to play varied parts.

Though actors who are currently making money

refuse to believe it, money seldom continues in an unbroken string. It's never wise to live up to your highest earning level without providing for the day when those bucks either shrink or disappear completely.

The third year after I became a full time actress, I made a lot of money in commercials. When I visited my accountant, he cautioned me about changing my lifestyle. *It won't last. Take your children on trips and enjoy it, but don't get a new apartment. I prepare actors' income tax returns all the time. It won't last.*

I'm conservative anyway, so I was fiscally careful, but I secretly thought he was wrong. I was different. I was just going to make more money every year. Sure!! Only two years later my income was down 66%.

Pretty humbling, but you know what? When I get a string of work — I *still* think there will be no more dry seasons. It's part of the human adaptive mechanism. Hope springs eternal!

How Much Should You Get Paid?

During that flush time, I had dinner one night with the producer of a soap on which I was appearing. The unspoken purpose of the dinner was for the producer to ascertain whether or not I was interested in joining his show as a regular before he would go back, find a place for me and make a real offer. During my first two years in the city, I had dreamt of such a job, but by the time of that dinner, I was already making enough money via commercials that the idea of being tied to a soap no longer appealed to me.

The producer wanted his information from the dinner and I wanted mine. I was curious to know how well my agent had negotiated for me. I had no way to measure whether the money she got for me was good, better or best.

The producer did me a big favor. He not only answered my question honestly, but he gave me a little education as well: *Part of being an actor is having that information yourself. You have to tell your agent what to ask for. You have to know what people are getting paid. You must know all the business ramifications as well.*

From that day forward, I've discussed money with other actors. I have the manuals available from each of the unions outlining pay scales. I make it a point to share information regarding what I am making and what others in the marketplace are making. If an actor never knows that his peers are capable of getting $1,500 or more for a day of work, he will never press for it.

Enhancing the Merchandise

Another part of your education includes knowing everything required to make you look good. It seems pretty astounding that the only people Cher thanked when she won her Academy Award were her makeup and hair people, but a large part of Cher's appeal is her visual impact. Cher's great style and single-minded focus on fulfilling that style emanates from her constantly in the form of charisma.

Successful movie stars know camera angles and understand everything about how they are lit in a scene. If you plan to make your living in front of a camera, get one and photograph everybody you know. Study the photos intently to see why one is more appealing than another. Get your own video camera, set it up and photograph yourself. Do a scene and see how your face looks from different angles and in different light.

A story that demonstrates how successful this approach can be involves Sara Purcell. Sara starred in a string of interview shows. The road to Sara's success was predictable, if you knew Sara. While working in a department store in San Diego, she got a chance to audition to be one of the hosts for a local talk show in Los Angeles called *AM/Los Angeles*. She found out on Friday about the audition for the following Monday. Luckily, she was then married to a man who directed local television commercials, was enormously creative, talented, and supportive, and owned a video camera in a time when most folks didn't.

All weekend they taped Sara interviewing their friends. They would tape, then sit back, look and critique. What worked? What didn't? How did she look when she moved a lot? A little? What was visually interesting? Everything, I guess, for Sara not only got the job, but an ongoing career.

Besides being very smart and enormously resourceful, Sara also has an innate sense of fun that's always apparent in her work. Those are the traits that she has enlarged upon to become a performer with a consistently successful track record.

The stars I know dedicate themselves single-mindedly to their careers. Are you prepared to do that?

Relationships

Don't forget about the people in your life. Actors have a reputation for being totally self-involved. It's hard not to be. We have to sell ourselves, assess where the next job is coming from, indulge our uniqueness, and deal with how our changing physicality is affecting our marketability. As a result, sometimes we get engrossed in ourselves and miss out on the really important things in life: family and friends. It takes creative energy to live a balanced life, it doesn't just happen.

When I started in the business, my children were young. Everyday, they waited anxiously for me to get home. They wanted to tell me everything about their day. They wanted to tell me who hit who. They wanted hugs and kisses. After a day out making rounds, all I really wanted to do was come home, get my messages, have a Dr. Pepper and relax.

Of course, I couldn't. They needed me. But, I couldn't really give them my undivided attention because I needed some time to myself. I hit upon what we called *re-entry time*. Kids can understand anything if you are straight about it. I explained that I needed 15 minutes when I first got home to deal with all phone calls, mail, etc.

When I got home they headed straight for the kitchen timer and set it for 15 minutes. When the bell rang, I had *re-entered the atmosphere* and was ready to give them my absolute attention. Actually, re-entry time turned out to be a pretty viable concept for all of our relationships and each of us has incorporated re-entry time into our lives to this day. There is a way to tend to business and pleasure.

All we have is today. Since the really successful people say the most fun was getting there, make sure you and your family enjoy the trip.

Wrap Up

✓ get a day job
✓ organize personal life
✓ make your living space comforting
✓ make a schedule
✓ establish and set aside workspace
✓ create physical and spiritual health
✓ provide for emotional needs
✓ form and nourish friendships
✓ get a mentor
✓ join or form a professional support group
✓ get in classes
✓ find a teacher not a guru
✓ be sure you retain your own belief systems
✓ practice informed viewing
✓ get a job in the business
✓ read books about the business
✓ educate yourself about handling money wisely
✓ learn union minimums and how to negotiate
✓ know your strong points and weaknesses

7   Self-Knowledge

People who are not working in the business are fond of saying: *It's not what you know, it's who you know.* I think I might rephrase that adage to say, *It's not what you know, it's how well you know your self.*

If you are your product, you'd better know all there is to know about your strengths and weaknesses.

✦   *Successful actors have an accurate image of what they sell. Unsuccessful actors don't. That's the sign. If you're getting the job, then you know who you are. If you're going out and you're not getting the job, then something is wrong. And you can't say it's talent. In this town, talent doesn't mean a lot. If you are the right type, you will get the job. I'm not saying you are going to get a* Hallmark Hall of Fame *signed contract, but you will be getting work.*

    You must always show your most commercial quality. They may or may not be looking for that essence that day, but one day they will and they will have already seen the one person who could do this better than anyone else in the world.

Martin Gage, agent
The Gage Group, Los Angeles

His East Coast counterpart, Phil Adelman had another way of saying it:

✦   *I had a funny-looking lady come in, mid-30s, chubby, not very pretty. For all I know, this woman could be brilliant. I asked her what roles she could play; what she thought she should get. She saw herself playing Sandra Bullock's roles. Meg Ryan's roles. I could have been potentially interested in this woman in the areas in which she would work. But it was a turn-off because, not only do I know that she's not going after the right things, so she's not preparing correctly, but she's not going to be happy with the kinds of things I'm going to be able to do for her. So I wouldn't want to commit to that person.*

It's easier for us to conceptualize that writers

bring a certain voice to the proceedings. Actors frequently think their job is to give a face to the scriptwriter's voice. The actor may not realize that he has been chosen to be the face of the material not just for his physical presence, but for his innate character and spirit.

Being Liked vs. Having a Voice

When you are so engaged in pleasing the prospective employer that your task becomes intuiting what he wants and seeking to give it to him, you mute your instrument.

Until that material passes through you and comes out processed by your own life experience, you have not added your contribution to the collaborative effort.

If you have no views, no life experience and no body of knowledge, you are restricting your potential.

I can still get in my own way at an audition. I hear what the buyer is looking for. The casting person gives me a direction (it may be a good one), but the instinct to please gets in the way of my evaluating it and making it my own before I take it and the result is not organic.

I saw Meryl Streep speaking on *Inside the Actor's Studio*, recently. She was discussing her work on a current film. She said she had forgotten how to act and could not even remember her lines.

When she spoke further about having been given a direction to emphasize this word instead of that, I had to smile. Of course she forgot her lines, she was no longer playing the through line, she was worrying about a word. Even Meryl Streep can get caught that way.

What an encouraging piece of information. I had just had an audition where I felt the same way. Not only had I not brought anything special to the table, I felt I had not acquitted myself well. Why? I didn't agree with the material. I intuited what I thought they wanted (not how I saw the material) and gave it to them that way.

Understand, I did not ask them what they had in

mind. My analysis of the script was that if the woman were in the situation they put her in, that she would behave much differently than the lines indicated.

I didn't feel that I should be giving notes to some of television's most highly acclaimed writers, but instead of just taking their lines and infusing them with the truth of what I felt (right or wrong) and giving a performance that was, at least, alive, I made the judgement that I no longer knew how to act and fulfilled that fantasy by doing a bad audition.

What Do You Like?

The more you perfect your own persona and trust your instincts, whether it is for what constitutes a really great pair of socks or a superb jump shot, the more you become the one you are. The great socks may not be great by someone else's standards, but what you are searching for are your socks and your jump shot.

If you can particularize your socks and your competition's socks, you'll have more understanding as to why one actor is chosen over another.

Analyze the people in your acting class. Try to perceive what they have to sell, not just what part they should play. What are their strengths and weaknesses?

After you've seen them work two or three times, try to imagine how they are going to approach their next scene. The more you are able to examine others, the more perfected that skill becomes for your own use.

Once you begin to successfully isolate your strengths and develop them, these attributes will take on a life of their own. There is an esoteric law of attraction: focus on your goal, do your work, live your life, the goal becomes yours.

When I moved to New York, I did everything I could lest I be mistaken for the middle-class lady from Texas I was. I wanted to be a sophisticated New Yorker.

What I didn't realize, Texas accent not withstanding, was that my very middle-classness is what I have to sell. I have played women who went to Vassar, but more often, they can and will get someone who actually went to Vassar for those parts.

Most acting teachers tell you that when you are looking for material, you should check out writers that come from your area of the country and your background because you will bring an innate truth to that material that no one else will be able to touch.

I'm an authentic lady from Texas who has raised three children and had various life experiences before, during and after. There is nobody else who has all of my particular components. If I don't prize what is uniquely me and find a way to tie that to a universality of the life experience, not only will I not work consistently and honestly, but my life will be a mess as well.

Susan Sarandon concurs:

✦ *All my mistakes in my roles and my life and all my self-explorations have put me in a good place. What I can bring to a part that no one else can is my life, my past.*

That's why I don't change my face or pretend to be younger. What I bring is what no 22-year-old can bring.
Singularly Susan
Bob Campbell
Sunday Republican
July 17, 1994

In another feature on Susan, she reiterates the value of experiencing real life.

✦ *I don't know how full a cup you can bring to a project if you're not living a life. If you're not drawing from real life, then all you're doing is rehashing images you've seen in films. Even the images of yourself. And all that doesn't interest me.*
She's Her Own Best Counsel
Gene Seymour
Los Angeles Times/Calendar
July 17, 1994

Andre Braugher who plays Frank Pembleton on NBC's *Homicide: Life on the Street*, is another who has taken heart from life's painful lessons and learned from them:

✦   *A graduate of Stanford University and Juilliard, Braugher received rave reviews for his performance as a rebellious slave in the hit 1989 film,* Glory. *In 1991, the New York based actor was told to come to Los Angeles because he was hot. Braugher waited and waited for the phone to ring. It didn't. So by year's end, he moved back to New York and soon got* Homicide.
     ...Braugher learned a lot from his L.A. experience. "This business is not going to keep me warm," Braugher says. "This business is not a priority. My priority is being a husband, a father, a son, a brother and a citizen. The lesson I learned back in 1991 was that I am not an actor. I am a man who acts. So consequently, everything that I need, everything important to me is about being a man."

> *When Race Isn't a Factor*
> Susan King
> *Los Angeles Times/TV Times*
> August 27, 1995

Getting To Know You

Independent Los Angeles agent Martin Gage (an ex-actor) and John Kimble from the William Morris Agency shared insights regarding self-discovery and distinctiveness:

✦   *Anything you can do to give you more of an idea of who you are, whether it's therapy, talking to people or looking in a mirror, that's valid.*
     There's an exercise I used to give my class when I taught actor therapy. I would tell them to get stark naked in front of a mirror and sit and look at themselves for an hour. Just sit and look at yourself. Look at how you look when you talk. When you move. Look at how your face changes. Look at how your body moves.
     The smart actor will study himself until he can see what it is that he has that is unique, special, commercial, saleable,

acceptable in him that he can develop and magnify and use better than anybody else.

Think of you and your four closest competitors. If someone sat and talked to each of you for 20 minutes, what would they see that was different? What is it about you? Why should they hire you instead of the other one? She may have more credits or make more money. Why should I hire you?

You have to go in with the qualities that are the most accessible of you to make those people buy you. When you walk in a room, you have about four seconds while people decide to hire or not hire you. It's your vibes.

They may call it your nose, but it's your vibes. You have to go in with the qualities that are the most accessible of you. You've got to get those people to buy you.

Martin Gage, agent
The Gage Group, Los Angeles

◆   *I believe every person on the face of the earth is unique. If I had a set of identical twins who were in touch with their uniqueness, I could sell them separately because, once they are in touch with their own uniqueness, there is no such thing as competition.*

A person's ideas dictate his uniqueness. What I believe about homosexuality or what I believe about any major subject is my uniqueness because it comes from my experience. So you can't compare it.

Many times you will be in the minority. The greatest people in the world have normally been in the minority.

John Kimble, agent
William Morris Agency, Los Angeles

◆   *This is what I am. This is what they want me to be. Can I put them together and find out what I am capable of being? They want me to be a nerd. I want to be sexy. Maybe I can be a sexy nerd. Then you have to convince your agent that this is who you are, because if your agent doesn't see it, you're out again.*

If the agent sees you and thinks he can make money on you, but not in the same way you think, then you have a problem. You and the agent must have the same vision. You might change his vision or he might change yours. If you both have the same vision, you'll be successful. The level of success may vary, but if you

*know who you are and the agent knows it, accurately, that's the
recipe for success.*

*And remember, what you are at 25 is not what you are at
35. Things change and your perception of yourself must change, too.*
Martin Gage, agent
The Gage Group, Los Angeles

Martin said the key words on the previous page:
develop and magnify. In the film, *Stage Door,* you have the
opportunity to see several star actresses at the beginning
of their careers before they developed and magnified
their respective uniquenesses. It's fascinating to see
Katharine Hepburn, Lucille Ball, Eve Arden and Ginger
Rogers in such an early stage of development.

Perhaps these women are not as familiar to you
as actors you routinely see on television, but if you do
know their later work, gleaning the kernel of what
became their ticket to stardom is an instructive process.

Other Factors

✦   *It's also a question of the competition. You can send a girl
in who's very pretty, does a great reading, but somebody else will
come in that happens to be a friend of the producer or a nephew of
the director or somebody that somebody wants to go to bed with.*

*There's 20,000 reasons why you're not going to get the
part. And it's not necessarily that you are without talent. It's
because there is so much competition. At the end of the week when I
see all the people I've gotten out on appointments, I say to myself,
"It's amazing that I did that. I'm just one little person." When I
think about all the agents and all the actors, I think we're lucky to
get people out on the appointment.*
Elinor Berger, agent
The Irv Schecter Agency, Los Angeles

✦   *The actor has got to have the creative energy juices flowing
and have the right mind set and the right attitudes to have the wins
come to him. He needs to have an angle on the role that's going to
be different and maybe the director is going to say, "That's*

interesting."

If the actor is not in his most creative time, he's going to miss some things. He's going to walk out of the audition and say, "Damn, I should have put this twist on it, or I don't know why I did that; it's so obvious."

If an actress' energies are in the theater, and she hasn't done a play in a year, it's going to drain her. She needs to be filled up and dealing with what to do about that. Equity Waiver, scene study, comedy workshop. There are choices; not just sit home and stare at the bare walls.

> Ann Geddes, agent
> *Geddes Agency,* Los Angeles

✦   *The winning difference between two actors on the same level auditioning for a role may just be that one makes everyone in the room have a better time.*

> Barry Freed, agent
> *Barry Freed Agency,* Los Angeles

So much for talent and training.

Dan Faucci, president of comedy development at Paramount Pictures, told me that when he was an actor, he met with two other actors three times a week for two hours to work on-camera, reading commercial copy and evaluating each other. I asked him if it helped him and if he began booking jobs. His answer:

✦   *Yes. We did book jobs, but I think it didn't matter whether or not we had the camera. It was the fact that we met three times a week focusing on what we wanted.*

Dan taught me a good exercise for beginning to get to know yourself. Spend 10 minutes communicating with yourself in the mirror. Do it by the clock. Just look at your face. Don't look for anything. You can look at your eyes, nose, lines, skin. See what you focus on. Don't judge it. Experience it. Take it in. If you start getting itchy at eight minutes, you're probably getting ready to feel something that is beginning to make you uncomfortable. Be brave: spend the full time and see what feelings come.

Assets and Liabilities

Make a list of all your skills. Your acting related skills, your entrepreneurial skills, everything you do well. Include making friends and staying positive if that's in your repertoire. These insights may take you further in your exploration.

How you work on the tasks we are speaking of delineates who you are. Your whole life is a laboratory to keep on looking at your way of working. If you procrastinate about your pictures and resumes, you are going to procrastinate about learning your lines.

Napoleon Hill writes in *Think and Grow Rich*, that every person has to conquer procrastination. Start now to do all your tasks the moment you think of them. As you work on the details of any project, you will work on every facet of your life. Begin to practice what you want your life to be.

Make a list of your liabilities. As you list drawbacks, perhaps you can formulate a plan to overcome them. If you think they're unsolvable problems, read Carol Burnett's biography.

There's no one in this business who could have been more disenfranchised than she was. If she could become successful against those odds, believe me, you have a chance *if* you can become that focused.

Hector Elizondo (who has worked for years, but finally became visible as the hotel manager in *Pretty Woman* and as Dr. Philip Watters on *Chicago Hope*) is a successful actor who has interesting things to say about hardship:

◆   *You can't really have style unless you've been someplace. I mean, you have to have been down. You have to have overcome something to have something. If you've had everything all your life, then you've never been tested and I don't think you're really the genuine article.*

You have to have come through something — because

that's how a sword is made. It's made from a piece of iron from the ground, and it's forged and beaten — that's the great metaphor for a human being. If you're born a sword, you aren't a real sword. But if you're forged from this iron ore — then comes this beautiful sword.

From Pretty Woman *to* Plenty Busy
Elias Stimac
Drama-Logue
Sept. 19-25, 1991

Jim Carrey is another example of tremendous success arising out of more than talent:

✦　　*I look at stuff that's happened in my life like it's* The Grapes of Wrath. *You know you'll always win in the end if you don't let the problems make you angry. I've been through some wild times. When my father lost his job and I was 13, we went from lower-middle class to complete poverty, living in a Volkswagen camper.*

　　My father was not good at business because he was too nice. I learned from that, not to be too nice when it comes down to the crunch. I definitely have an edge because of all that. But nothing made me go, 'Life sucks, people suck'.

　　I now want to make sure that my daughter Jane's financial future is as secure as I can possibly make it. That I'll be able to look after myself when I'm old. That drives me. Definitely.

　　I've always believed in magic. When I wasn't doing <u>anything</u> in this town, I'd go up every night, sit on Mulholland Drive, look out at the city, stretch out my arms and say, 'Everybody wants to work with me. I'm a really good actor. I have all kinds of great movie offers.'

　　I'd just repeat these things over and over, literally convincing myself that I had a couple of movies lined up. I'd drive down that hill, ready to take the world on, going, 'Movie offers are out there for me. I just don't hear them yet.'

　　It was like total affirmations, antidotes to the stuff that stems from my family background, from knowing how things can go sour. Still, I've had times that, when I'd walk down the street, I'd look at the street people and feel like, 'I'm already one of them. I'm already there.' I mean, I can scare the shit out of myself.

... I've always believed that everything I've wanted, prayed for, will come to me in one way or another. I'm real careful about what I ask for. I asked God when I was young to give me whatever I need to help me be a great actor-comedian.

So, okay, it's like now you're going to be poverty-stricken, now you're going to go through a divorce. I've always seen these things as, 'This is a rock in my way for me to learn how to get over'. Like, I expected to get on Saturday Night Live, *do that trip, but that didn't happen. But I got on* In Living Color. *You may not always get where you expected but, so long as you're somewhere, who cares?*

Carrey'd Away
Stephen Rebello
Movieline
July 1994

It's possible that you must come from a background of great pain to have that kind of drive. My personal bias is that a balanced person would not have the drive to be a star in any field because he would not have that desperate need to prove himself.

Debra Winger thinks success is about being available to the camera:

✦   *In a word, openness. Openness of the heart, of the soul. The camera is open. Many people are not. A director can spend a whole day setting up a shot, getting the angles just right, the lighting perfect; but visually, if the actor isn't open, it's a dead end. It's got nothing to do with physical beauty either. You can shoot identical twins; if one is open and one is closed, the one twin will resonate on film and the closed one won't.*

Confessions of a Reluctant Sex Goddess
Tom Robbins
Esquire
February 1993

Focusing On What You Have To Sell

Knowing what you have to sell does not

necessarily mean always preparing yourself to play the same part, but preparing to focus on the energy that will alert the casting director to your strength.

If you consistently play banker types, it's probable that you have an innate fastidiousness that is associated with detail oriented people. If you exaggerate and develop this trait, you might be the first thought for any casting executive who is casting these roles.

Look carefully to see how you fit in with actors who are being bought. In situation comedies, there is usually a next door neighbor (man, woman or both) who is zanier, less pretty/handsome than the lead. Frequently there is an acerbic, scratchy quality to contrast the lead.

The lead needs to be more bland than the supporting players in order to create the perfect balance. When you make a cake, flour (bland) is the chief ingredient followed in quantity (but not importance) by the liquid (the binder) and the spices. The flour holds it all together and the spices add zip, but too much vanilla or sugar or salt (without which the project or cake would be inedible) would render the effort useless as well.

In adventure/detective shows, there's usually a hard-boiled chief that is at odds with the hero. And of course, there are always exotic bad guys and white trash bad guys and corporate bad guys. If you can come up with a new twist on the bad guy, you can really be in demand. Commercials feature the dumb one (with the problem) and the smart one (who solves the problem).

When I was guesting on a show called *It's a Living,* I had a conversation with it's star, Ann Jillian. She has just had a mastectomy. During chemotherapy she amassed a wardrobe of wigs in order to maintain the look her buyers had come to expect. She told me that she felt that once you are lucky enough to establish an image, it's important to keep it.

Knowing When To Change

Even though the search for a professional

identity is critical, it is an ongoing process. And it changes. Donna Mills' image originally was as a passive, adorable, trustworthy blonde instead of the evil, spiteful and conniving Abbey she became on *Knots Landing*

Donna decided that she wanted that part and went for it. David Jacobs, producer of *Knots,* told me her agent called and wanted her considered for the part. Her agent was told: *Okay, we know Donna. We'll consider her.*

No, no, retorted Donna's agent. *She wants to come in and read for the part.*

The producers were blown away by the reading. In fact, their idea of Donna's image at that time would have kept them from seriously considering her for the part had she not insisted on being seen.

Calling and insisting to be read was a very Abbey thing to do. Abbey was a lady who got what she wanted. It isn't just that Donna put on more exotic make-up and turned into Abbey. Obviously, her adjustment to life changed, too.

It's Never Over

Happily, it's never over. We don't ever finish learning to act. I wonder if any professional ever finishes studying. A brain surgeon learns a particular procedure one day, but if he doesn't continually practice and refine the technique, he won't be the brain surgeon everyone wants. If he does not continue to read, search and study, he will not maintain his superiority. Neither the actor nor the surgeon will prosper without enjoying and practicing the continuity of process.

All we have is now. If you are not fulfilled by the now, get out of the business. If the payoff for you is a Tony, an Oscar, or big bucks, change jobs now. You will miss your whole life waiting for the prize. If you are unfortunate enough to get the prize while in this mind-set, you will find you are the same unhappy person you were the day before you got your statue.

I once heard an interview on the radio with Desi

Arnaz, Jr., a young actor who had it all for all intents and purposes. He said:

✦   *Yes, it did seem like I had it all. Except that's not 'it'. I had the car, the house, the position and I was terribly unhappy. I got into alcohol and drugs. That wasn't 'it' either. There's really no difference between me and the people who have nothing...who think 'it' is all those things.*

        They, at least, think if they had a big career and all the things money can buy, they would be happy. Imagine how depressing it is to have all those things and still be unhappy?

Self Indulgence

It's up to you and how smart you are, how you make positive choices, how you focus, how you ask for what you want and how you don't let yourself sink into negative thinking. It's absolutely self indulgent to allow yourself to think all those self destructive thoughts actors leap to given the barest opportunity:

- *Oh, I'll never get a job*
- *Oh, I'll never get a job again*
- *Nobody wants me*
- *I'm no good*

Not only does nobody want to hear you talk like that and/or be around you in that frame of mind, but that thinking only drains your energy and prolongs your pain. Don't cut yourself off from your feelings. You don't have to go into denial, go ahead and acknowledge the pain and then go for a walk.

Spend time with yourself. Explore. Use the meditation time I spoke about to just be. Gain perspective. This business is a constant test for maintaining perspective.

Write about it. Writing is a magical exercise. At my most depressed moments, when I can remember to write about it, the feelings go from my brain through the pencil to the paper and I feel better.

If you enjoy being unhappy, then keep thinking about your pain. You have the ability to turn your mind to something else. If you don't refocus on something else and put your energy into something positive, we have to assume you would rather be unhappy.

Learning about yourself can be a painful experience, but the payoff is worth it. I remember one point in my life when I realized that the one constant in all the unhappy relationships I had ever been involved in, was me.

That was pretty depressing until I realized that was good news. If the problem was the other people, there was nothing I could do about it. But, if it was me, I could set about changing it.

Wrap Up

✓   know which one you are
✓   assess your assets and liabilities
✓   explore what makes you special
✓   choose mentors and role models
✓   analyze the marketplace
✓   allow yourself to hear your voice
✓   ongoing depression is self-indulgent
✓   defining oneself is a lifetime process

8   Stand-Up Comedy/One-Person Shows

Many of today's biggest film and television successes entered the business as stand-up comedians. Jim Carrey, Whoopi Goldberg, Ray Romano (*Everybody Loves Raymond*), Robin Williams, Billy Crystal and Paul Reiser are just a few of the entrepreneurs who started either as stand-ups or in their own one-person shows.

The rewards of creating your own work are rich indeed: Jim Carrey will make $20 million for his next film and the amount of money Jerry Seinfeld generated with his show has entered the pages of television financial lore.

The skills you develop writing, producing and performing your own stand-up act can move you toward varying careers as evidenced by a stand-up team of some years ago — Craig T. Nelson and Barry Levinson. Nelson starred in many successful theatrical films before settling into ABC's long-running sitcom, *Coach* and Levinson has written and/or directed *Good Morning Vietnam, The Natural, Diner* and *Bugsy* among other films.

The road to the bank is, however, precarious and they don't give just anyone the key. An in-depth feature by David Kronke on making it as a stand-up reports that patience and a work ethic are the keys to success:

✦   *It's a long trek, economically at least, from the comedy clubs to a hit TV series.*

Ask Paul Reiser. "You started at nothing, coming to the city, then you'd work your way up to $5 a night, $20 a weekend, $50 for a gig here and there, with luck, you could put that together and you'd get enough to pay the rent....Certainly no one goes into comedy for the money. You can't make money."

The Big Payoff
David Kronke
Los Angeles Times/Calendar
July 23, 1995

At this point I'd like to remind you of the statistics discussed in chapter two: in 1997 67% of the members of Screen Actors Guild earned less than $3,000. It's not just comics that starve. Anyone who goes into the business for the money is buying a very big lottery ticket. You've got to be in the business because you love being in the business — rain or shine.

If you were to apply the same amount of time and creative energy pursuing any other kind of work, you would have a better return on the investment.

That said, here's the way to begin, if you want to become a stand-up.

Put together a stand-up act. If there are no comedy clubs in your area (which seems unlikely), call local service organizations like The Lions Club and The Jaycees. They are always looking for entertaining speakers for their functions. Charge at least $50, and remember, the more they pay you, the more they respect you.

Putting together an act is not as formidable as it seems. Just do it one joke at a time. A way to build material is to sit down and make a list of things that make you angry: the guy who parks in the handicapped zone while you obey the rules, people who cut in front of you on the freeway, the guy who steals what would have been your parking place, shoppers who speed up just enough to beat you to the checkout line at the grocery store, etc.

There's a universality of humor in all our pet peeves. Tap into that. Get one minute together, then five. Test the jokes out on your friends (but don't tell them you're auditioning your material), then volunteer to be master of ceremonies at some function and try out your material. When you have 20 minutes —- call comedy clubs and get hired.

Perhaps you could be the weather forecaster on your local television station. Weathermen/women in the major markets are frequently cast from the ranks of stand-up comedians. As a matter of fact, stand-up comedians are considered such ripe potentials for television situation comedies, casting directors from Los Angeles regularly monitor comedy club operations all over the country.

Adam Carolla is the co-host of the nationally syndicated sex-themed radio show, *Loveline*. How did someone with a background as a day laborer end up in with a job mixing jokes and advice on sex and relationships?

✦   *Lacking connections and self-confidence, Carolla made a deal with himself that by the time he turned 30, he could make a living doing comedy. He spent the next 10 years supplementing construction work with small gigs: teaching comedy traffic school, performing at office parties and doing skits with the Acme Improv and Groundlings theater groups.*

Two weeks before turning 30, he heard KROQ morning jocks Kevin and Bean talking about a boxing match between two on-air personalities.

"It hit me like a ton of bricks," Carolla said. As a longtime boxer who worked as a trainer between construction jobs, he figured he was perfect for the job of preparing one of the participants to fight.

Mixing Ribald and Real Life
Dade Hayes
The Los Angeles Times
March 5, 1998

Training the boxers led to an appearance on the show as the continuing character, Mr. Birthum, a cantankerous shop teacher whose repertoire included heavy tools and sexual innuendo.

Dr. Drew Pinsky, the creator of *Loveline* became a fan of Birthum's and he mentioned Carolla to his producers who were looking for a new co-host. The marriage of Pinsky and Carolla has produced a show that mixes the doctor's establishment voice with Carolla's irreverence. Carolla is living proof of what he believes, *My take on the universe is that it's not evil and it's not kind. It's not anything. You get exactly as far as your talent and motivation can take you.*

What It Takes

Producing your own stand-up act or one-person show doesn't necessarily take much money, but it does take a sense of humor and writing knowhow. If you have not perfected your writing skills yet, get on with it.

John Kretchmer was directing an episode of *Lois & Clark* when I tracked his path for my book, *Directing Your Directing Career*. His pragmatic approach can teach us all a lesson.

Organized and smart, John set about researching his employment possibilities and learning the business by working in a variety of jobs on the sets of various films and television shows.

He worked as a production assistant, a prop man and in craft services hustling food for entire sets of cast and crew. Armed with his own firsthand analysis of job possibilities, as soon as John was sure that he wanted to be a director, he made a wise decision. Knowing that a good script is the director's first step and knowing that he didn't have any option money, he determined to take a year off and learn to write.

He learned pretty well, since one of his plays was read at the prestigious O'Neill Playwrights Foundation in New York and another was a finalist at the Sundance Institute. Although he didn't get his first directing gig via his own material, the single-minded focus on his goal placed him in fortunes path and Stephen Spielberg became his mentor.

My own personal bias is that if you can write, you can cross over many lines. There may be many jokes about the lack of power in the writers' career, but the truth is that if you can write your own material, particularly if you can write your own *funny* material, you can begin to be in charge of your own destiny. Stand-up is a good place to gather skills and experience without waiting for someone else to choose you.

Comedy Club Salaries

Club Comics are remunerated in proportion to their fame in a given area. "Craig Shoemaker is a phenomenal draw in regions where he's been a staple, and he can bring in $15,000 a short week — but in the Midwest, where he has less exposure, he may only bring in $4,500," says Improv booking agent Robert Hartman.

"Salaries vary according to ticket sales and whether the club can sell tickets on Tuesday, Wednesday and Thursday," Hartman adds. At 300 seats, for four shows at $20 a ticket, a headliner act can get 50% of the gross [$12,000] and maybe bonuses too. A name act who plays a five-show weekend at the Los Angeles Improv negotiates a salary based on the $17 ticket price and 300 seats, which creates a gross profit of $25,000. Middle-liners can get up to $5,000 a week and are booked for several consecutive weeks, while MCs who often have the most demanding job in the house, currently only receive $75-$100 per set.

"Salaries on the road peaked about three years ago," according to comic Rhonda Shear, who has hosted 400 episodes of USA's Up All Night. *"A lot of people who were making $4,000 a week on the road three years ago are only getting $1,200-1,500," Shear reports. The new club scene seems to be the cruise ships, which pays the same top acts $4,000-$5,000.*

Comedy Club Salaries
Brooke Comer
The Hollywood Reporter Comedy Special
March 3, 1998

Character/A Special Voice

Wherever you establish your developmental beachhead, your goal is not simply to make money, but to create a character that is your own. If you can do that, you will have the option of taking your creation into a larger venue than your own home town.

✦   *Kim Fleary, vice-president for comedy series development at ABC Entertainment, says that to score big, what a comic needs most is "a point of view and an infectious personality."*

The Big Payoff
David Kronke
Los Angeles Times/Calendar
July 23, 1995

Though the comedy club craze has peaked, there
are still venues in which to practice your skills:

✦ *A lot of comedy clubs have closed across the country, but
there are still a fair amount in the Northeast so it's easier to keep a
comic working there as they start to develop. The more stage time
they get, they better they become. We encourage them to get into
acting classes, not to become actors, but just to start. We want to
know what their long-range goals are. In order for a comic to become
popular, he needs television exposure. If you can support that with a
strong act, you're going to have a good career.*
Tom Ingegno, agent
Omnipop, New York

✦ *We've definitely steered toward a very personality oriented
comic. A charismatic style comic.* The Tonight Show *might use a
comic because they're a very good comic in terms of their writing —
a structural comic who writes a perfect setup and a punch line. Some
of those comics wouldn't cross over into a sitcom because they might
just be joke tellers. We want somebody who is a very full bodied
character a la Roseanne, Tim Allen or Seinfeld. The development
and casting people are looking for that. They are already walking in
with a character. Some comics have stronger skills in that area.*
Bruce Smith, agent
Omnipop, Los Angeles

✦ *A comedic person has to have the backing of theatrical
training, otherwise you're looking at a personality-oriented project.
Many stand-ups came out of theater and did stand-up as a means
of survival.*
Steve Tellez, agent
CAA, Los Angeles

✦ *I wouldn't assume that just because you are a comedic
actor that you can do stand-up. Soap opera people try to do stand-*

up. Most of them, since they are so pretty have not lived that angst ridden life that comics have. It becomes a frivolous version of comedy. The first thing you want to establish with an actor that is going into comedy is: Do they have a natural feel for it? Do they have comedic rhythm for it? There are many actors who are wonderful with comedy, but can't do stand-up. You need the stage time.

> Bruce Smith, agent
> *Omnipop, Los Angeles*

Jim Carrey might appear to be an overnight success, but he has been perfecting his talents for 15 years in an extremely focused and businesslike way:

✦   *A native of the Toronto area, Carrey went professional in 1980, ultimately developing a reputation for his ability to do impressions, with a repertoire of 100-plus characters. After moving to Los Angeles, he became a regular at the Comedy Store, where he honed his skills. In 1982, he landed the lead role in the NBC midseason sitcom* Duck Factory, *a show that was quickly pulled. He then took a two-year sabbatical from stand-up to take acting lessons:*

"I saw where it was going. I was going to end up some kind of comedy phantom in Vegas, doing some kind of tribute show. It was so confining creatively, because I had all these weird ideas that I could never use, because it didn't fit into the act. I just got tired of it. I wanted to be an original. That's all."

> *Jim Carrey*
> David Pecchia
> *The Hollywood Reporter*
> *1994 Comedy Special Issue*/July 26, 1994

The personal appearance agents that I spoke to in New York and Los Angeles supported what I have learned from theatrical agents and scriptwriters' agents: established agents are mostly not interested in one-shot representation. Many unrepresented actors (directors, writers, etc.) think that if they land a job on their own (even a development deal) and call up an agent to handle it for them, that the agent will welcome them with open arms. The agent is going to make money, right?

That's not how it goes. The agent is interested in a client with a body of work that shows growth and development, not what might be just a lucky incident in a young career.

If you lived in Los Angeles and got a guest shot on *Drew Carey* and called an agent with that shot as an entree, he would probably take your call, but if you don't have a track record of credits (they don't all have to be as important as *Drew Carey*), then the credible agent would not be interested. Ten percent of an episode is not enough for him to put you on his list to share all his introductions and hard work.

If you have written a one-person show and Disney is interested, that may or may not be interesting to a stand-up agent. Development deals go south with regularity and if you don't already have a stand-up career going for yourself, personal appearance agents won't be. They want people who have been playing clubs in and out of town and have the stage time.

◆   *This is Wendy Liebman's 10th year as a stand-up; she moved to Los Angeles four years ago to pursue it fulltime. This year, she was a nominee in the best female stand-up category of the American Comedy Awards.*

...'I've always done things in my own time. When I moved out here, I just knew I wasn't ready. I wasn't that anxious either. I knew I had to get some acting classes under my belt. The thing about stand-up, I know I can go into Caesar's Palace and open for Julio Iglesias or Ann-Margaret and feel comfortable doing it. I feel like I could do any stand-up anywhere because I've done it. But acting, it took me a while to feel comfortable there. To say out loud that I'm ready is the first step. From there, people can say yes or no, but I'm ready.'

Next on the Stand-Up to TV Circuit
David Kronke
The Los Angeles Times
May 27, 1995

A career as a stand-up is a bonafide way get up in front of people quickly, but there are no short-cuts to acting or comedic maturity. You gotta do the time.

Once you are ready, several companies and studios are pioneering a way for young comics to be seen:

✦ *As a way of providing a showcase for their clients and perhaps offering a glimpse into the future of programming, several companies and studios have turned to alternative outlets like cable. CAA launched a weekly series* (Limboland) *featuring its clients on cable's* Comedy Central. *Others are following suit, most notably Messina-Baker Entertainment.*

Its program Small Doses *is being funded by Viacom in exchange for options on the talent and concepts. The sketchlike format, featuring a collection of mini-programs that are prototypes for would-be series, is being made at low costs.*

Character Building
Rick Sherwood
The Hollywood Reporter
1994 Comedy Special Issue
July 26, 1994

Comedy Clubs

Since successful comedians breed successful and visible comedy clubs, smart club owners in Los Angeles are known to give a helping hand to developing comics:

✦ *Club owners such as Jamie Masada (Laugh Factory), Mitzi Shore (The Comedy Store) and Budd Friedman (The Improvization) don't just book comics; they also help them with their acts. "We work them out and place them and watch them grow," the Comedy Store's Shore says. "It's like a gym."*

"We're obligated as club owners to keep feeding the industry with talent and train them and make them ready," adds Masada, who co-manages Harlan Williams, the 32-year-old star of the WB Network's upcoming sitcom, Simon *about a Forrest Gump-like character.*

Launching Pads
Connie Benesch
The Hollywood Reporter Comedy Special Issue
July 25, 1995

Comedian Referral Service/ Rent a Comic

The Comedyzine Referral Service is a free online listing for comedians, agents, managers and publicists. Each listing links you to their site. If you need to hire a comedian for a corporate, college or other function, you can select the comedian by going directly to their site, or their agent's site.

If you are a comedian, agent, manager, or publicist, and wish to be listed, you can E-mail your URL address to: listings@comedyzine.com including your city, state/province and country. There is no charge, but you must have a web page for them to link to.

One-Person Shows

If you don't see yourself as a stand-up artist, but have the drive and ability to produce a one-person show, you might want to consider putting one together. Even if you don't attract someone who sees your act as a pilot for a situation-comedy, if you have a point of view and are well produced, you might well have an annuity that can be booked across the country into college venues.

It's not a new idea and it's not reserved just for new talent trying to break in. Lynn Redgrave's *Shakespeare For My Father* has been playing across the country for several years and *Star Trek*'s Patrick Stewart's production of *A Christmas Carol* has become a seasonal Broadway attraction.

As successful a venue as stand-up has been, some feel one-person shows may be the way to go:

✦   *With the economic trouble the stand-up world has found itself in, people are taking their act and shaping it into one-person*

*shows. The industry is now looking to solo performers as artists who
are not only funny but have also fashioned a way to present that
theatricality in an entertaining way.*

*.....and Claudia Shear, whose hysterical one-woman
account of her working world struggles,* Blown Sideways
Through Life, *is now inundated with book and feature film
deals.*

*While Shear noted that the solo show is nothing new, she
was completely unprepared for the 'tsunami of publicity' that
followed when* Blown Sideways *opened off-Broadway in the fall of
'94. "It's become more acceptable to hear the one voice — it's a very
elemental connection with people — saying, 'This is what happened
to me tonight'," explains Shear, who does not consider herself a solo
performer nor a comedienne, even though her show has been widely
perceived as such.*

Hittin' the Boards
Rachel Fischer
The Hollywood Reporter Comedy Special Issue
July 25, 1995

Filling the Stage

It so hard to get into the business sometimes that
a performer forgets that the agents, producers, networks,
cruise ships, colleges, film companies — everyone who
hires performers — all really need the performers as
much as the performers need the bookings. There are
many stages to fill, whether that stage is on a sound stage
or at a comedy club. If you are any good at all and have
the creativity, drive and stamina to move forward on your
own, there will be those who will see your energy and try
to attach themselves to it.

Assuming that you plan to make the necessary
investment of your time, energy and entrepreneurial
spirit, decide now to take yourself seriously. Resolve to
grade your work as you would any other performer's. Just
because you get a job, don't assume that means your cake
is baked, it only means you have a job:

✦   *"The danger comes when the comedian isn't ready but he thinks he is because they put him on a contract," says the Laugh Factory's Masada. "He thinks he knows it all, and instead of developing his comedy, he's relaxing, living in a dream that they're going to make him a star."*
        The Big Payoff
        David Kronke
        Los Angeles Times/Calendar
        July 23, 1995

✦   *But even getting the order for a network series does not mean that a stand-up comic has cleared the final hurdle. For many reasons — a difficult time slot, a mistranslation of comic persona, a lack of acting skills — even the most highly touted vehicle can founder. Last season, for instance, the Korean-American comic Margaret Cho's* All-American Girl *was a huge disappointment for ABC. Industry consensus is that Ms. Cho, still in her 20s, had nowhere near the show-business savvy or corporate support needed to turn her sassy observational humor into the ground breaking sitcom that critics and viewers were expecting.*
        Looking for Laughs in a Grim Race to Prime Time
        Andy Meisler
        The New York Times
        August 27, 1995

You are the one who is going to make you a star. Because there is such a fine line between the kind of arrogance it takes to get up and believe in yourself and the kind of arrogance that blinds itself to criticism, you can't afford to sip the drug of self-satisfaction. Your focus has to be about fulfilling the work; otherwise, when the money people want to change you, you won't have the strength to stay true to yourself. A true picture of your contribution only emerges over time. Take the time to become.

✦   *Indeed comics' and networks' expectations can be exasperatingly at odds. Comics are hired because of their distinctive outlooks and perspectives, but then the networks will sometimes try to shoehorn them into premises antithetical to their nature and saddle them with writers and executive producers who don't understand their appeal.*

"The nature of TV development is that there is this tremendous ambivalence on the part of networks — they want something new and different, yet they feel most comfortable with what's tried and true," [Paul] Reiser says. "Had Seinfeld *not had the process it had, going through NBC's late-night division, it never would have gone. They'd have just said, 'What is* this *about?'"*

> The Big Payoff
> David Kronke
> *Los Angeles Times / Calendar*
> July 23, 1995

Craig Shoemaker is a successful stand-up who spent much of the 1980s on the road. In the late '80s, NBC signed him to a development deal and he found himself auditioning in the office of Brandon Tartikoff.

✦ *"All of a sudden, I couldn't act to save my life," Shoemaker says. "I was supposed to do a scene on the phone to someone. When I'd rehearsed it, I'd pantomime the phone, but this time I picked up the real phone that was sitting there. There was someone on the line and he was yelling at me to get off.*

"...The wrenching experience served as a dividing line," he says. Shortly afterward, Mr. Shoemaker swore off alcohol and drugs, blaming them for his lack of focus, and became more serious about his comedy: "I realized that I'd been so involved in the results, I hadn't been into the work itself."

> Looking for Laughs in a Grim Race to Prime Time
> Andy Meisler
> *The New York Times*
> August 27, 1995

Roseanne's book, *My Lives,* details the battles she had to fight in order to get her work onto the television screen and in a *New York Times* interview, Brett Butler agreed:

✦ *...unless you're willing to put yourself on the line every single day you're doing this, you might as well just stay home.*

Looking for Laughs in a Grim Race to Prime Time
Andy Meisler
The New York Times
August 27, 1995

Margaret Cho learned the hard way:

✦   *Be really stubborn. Know as much as you can about what you want, because you'll be pulled this way and that...Stick to your guns, even though it's really difficult.*
   The Big Payoff
   David Kronke
   Los Angeles Times/Calendar
   July 23, 1995

Margaret's advice is pertinent no matter what you do. Learning how to get along with all the other collaborators but being able to hold onto your voice at the same time is an art.

If you're just doing stand-up with you and a stool and a microphone, you don't need anyone else except sound and lighting to make an impact, but when you venture onto a larger stage, you and your collaborators must be in sync.

Wrap Up

✓   successful stand-ups get the key to the bank
✓   patience and work ethic are necessary
✓   most stand-ups don't make money
✓   the road is long and challenging
✓   writing ability and sense of humor are essential
✓   character and viewpoint are necessary
✓   one-person shows can have a big impact
✓   need to be strong, flexible and have a unique voice
✓   stick to your guns

9   Children in the Business

Children have no business giving up their childhoods to be actors. They are not in a position to make such a costly judgement about their lives. You only get to be a kid once. If you don't experience childhood at the appropriate time, you will never get a legitimate shot at it again.

I urge any parent who is considering letting their child earn some easy money to pay for their college tuition with *a few commercials now and then, maybe an episode or two on television or maybe even a play*, to really think again. Management pays a child as much money per day as an adult and expects the child to perform as an adult, no matter what.

And what if things get out of hand and your child becomes the new Macauley Caulkin? Can you or your child turn your back on all that money and adulation just so he can play football and be a normal kid?

That said, my interview with successful stage mother/manager, now children's agent, Judy Savage pretty well shot all my arguments full of holes.

✦   *Kids who have problems in the business came from dysfunctional families in the first place. It's not necessarily that the business goes to the children's heads, it goes to the parents' heads. I don't think the number of showbiz kids who become messed up is any greater than the general public, but you hear about them because they are so visible and they have a little more money for drugs.*

Judy Savage
Judy Savage Agency

Judy's philosophy explains why her clients and her own kids ended up not only working, but being productive grown-ups as well:

✦   *I think it's a great business and that you can pay for your braces, your caps, your car, your wedding, your house, and hopefully go on in the business or in some other aspect of life with a good start.*

Treat it as a hobby that you are lucky enough to get paid for, it's not going to go on forever. You can count on your two hands the number of actors whose careers who go on for 40-50 years. The average career is five years for all members of Screen Actors Guild.

Judy Savage
Judy Savage Agency

Elizabeth Taylor's early life as a child actor is not one that she recommends:

✦   *Looking back, I think I missed not having a childhood, not going to a regular school. I had a lot of fathers and avuncular friends on the set. They were great. They used to throw me around and play baseball with me and sneak me candy and comic books. But it wasn't the same as having peers, and I think I would advise parents of child actors not to push it. It's a hard life for a child not to have a childhood. It's rough.*

Pearls of Wisdom from Liz
Charles Champlin
The Los Angeles Times
March 31, 1996

Don't Put All Your Kids' Eggs in One Basket

If your child is serious about pursuing a career in show business, in addition to studying acting, I would encourage him to exercise his entrepreneurial skills, so that when he gets out of school, he will be truly prepared. The newspapers are full of the stories about the troubles of ex-child stars who will never get their lives back because they did not prepare for their future.

Career Span

Let's speak realistically about age and aging. Even you babies under 20 or 30 should read this. I know you

can't conceive of ever being 40 or 50 or even, God
forbid, 60, but if you are lucky, you will be.

If you are a kid and want to work in the business,
take note. Your life expectancy in the business is 5 years,
10 years tops. While you are on the set missing growing
up like a normal kid, playing ball, having dates and going
to the prom, you are getting a lot of attention, money and
perqs. You get to go special places and people ask for
your autograph.

Once you hit the later teen years, it may well be all
over. Carrie Fisher, daughter of Eddie Fisher and Debbie
Reynolds wrote and narrated a special on A&E called
Carrie Fisher — The Hollywood Family. It was an
illuminating hour about many aspects of life in the
business. There was nothing more upsetting than the
segment dealing with child actors.

Paul Peterson spent his childhood on *The Donna
Reed Show*. When parts stopped coming his way, he got
into trouble with drugs and the law. Today, he is clean
and has dedicated himself to helping kids whose careers
didn't make it past age 18. On Carrie's show, you see
Paul visiting Anthony Thompkins, a former child star
from the show, *Diff'rent Strokes*. He visited Anthony in
prison where he is doing time for drugs and burglary.
Anthony said:

✦   *Nobody sat me down and said, 'Well, look out. You are 12
years old now, but when you're 18, you'd better watch out, because
work is going to dry up.' If they'd told me that, I would have been
prepared for it.*

*By not accepting the fact that I could expand, that there was
something else I could do, that's how I ended up here.*
Carrie Fisher — The Hollywood Family
Arts & Entertainment Television
August 13, 1995

Actually, I doubt that if he had been told, he would
have believed his career would not last. It's hard to
believe you won't be darling forever. Facing rejection and
unavailability of parts for people in his age range played

an important role in the downward spiral that put him in jail. He's not the only one. Fellow cast members, Todd Bridges and Dana Plato followed a similar path.

On the special, we see Peterson drive away from the prison talking about kids and their fantasies *Of course kids want to be actors. They want to be baseball stars and football stars, too. What's the window of opportunity for child actors? 5 years? 10 years? How long are you an adult? 40 years? By pursuing something so limited in time, you're foreclosing your options for professional achievement for 40-50 years. That a bad deal. And all of this comes at the expense of homework and socialization skills.*

Carrie Fisher closes the show saying:

✦ *Celebrity can never be a career, it's too fleeting; but by the time that the kid actor realizes that learning lines is no substitute for learning, it's too late. They have nothing to fall back on when Hollywood gets sick of them and drops them without even a gold watch.*

Carrie Fisher — The Hollywood Family
Arts & Entertainment Television
August 13, 1995

If you are a parent reading this, the following information regarding child labor laws as specified in the California Labor Code may be helpful to you. If you live in another state, you might want to use this as your guide. It is up to you to protect your child. All management cares about is getting the film in the can.

Working Hours

✦ *The number of hours minors are permitted at the place of employment within a 24-hour period is limited according to age. Travel time must be considered working time.*

Babies under fifteen days old are not permitted to work.

Babies fifteen days to six months old may be on the set no more than two hours, but may work no more than twenty minutes.

Babies six months to two years may be on the set for four hours, but may work no more than two hours, the balance of time reserved for rest and recreation.

Children two to six years old may be on the set for six hours, but may work no more than three hours, the balance of time is reserved for rest and recreation.

Children six to nine years old may be on the set for eight hours. When school is in session, they may work only four hours and must receive three hours of schooling with one hour for rest and recreation. When school is not in session, they may work six hours, the balance to be used for rest and recreation.

Children from nine to sixteen years old may be on the set for nine hours. When school is in session, they may work five hours and must receive three hours of schooling with the balance to be used for rest and recreation. When school is not in session, they may work seven hours, the balance to be used for rest and recreation.

Children from sixteen to eighteen years old may be on the set for ten hours. When school is in session, they may work six hours and must receive three hours of schooling with the balance to be used for rest and recreation. When school is not in session, they may work eight hours, the balance for rest and recreation.

All minors under sixteen years of age: A studio teacher must be provided and has the responsibility for caring and attending to the health, safety and morals of the minor. For babies fifteen days to six weeks, a nurse must be present. A parent or guardian must be present on the set or location for all minors.

All minors under eighteen years of age must have a permit to work issued by the Labor Commissioner and their employers must also obtain a permit to employ. These permits are not required if the minor is sixteen or seventeen and is a high school graduate or has a certificate of proficiency.

California laws apply when a California employer takes a resident minor out of state.

The hours at the place of employment as shown above may be extended by no more than one-half hour for meal periods.

Twelve hours must elapse between the minor's time of dismissal and time of call on the following day.

For purposes of the California labor code, the entertainment industry is defined as: Any organization, or individual, using the services of any minor in: motion pictures of any type (film, videotape, etc.), using any format (theatrical, film, commercial, documentary, television program, etc.), photography, recording, theatrical

productions, publicity, rodeos, circuses, musical performances and
any other performances where minors perform to entertain the
public.

Baby Talk
David Robb
Daily Variety
June 26, 1991

Screen Actors Guild publishes an informative free booklet available to young actors called the *AFTRA-SAG Young Performers Handbook.* This booklet deals with everything from dressing rooms to child labor laws and details all the contracts the young performer might work under.

The handbook also lists the names and addresses of the departments of labor in every state as well as for Canada.

The *YPH* is available to SAG members in person or by mail from the guild and is published in its entirety on the SAG website: http://www.sag.com/youngpersons.html

If you live in Los Angeles, SAG holds a special *Young Performers Orientation* that occurs the third Tuesday of each month at 7 p.m. in the James Cagney Room on the first floor of the Guild headquarters at 5757 Wilshire Blvd. Current labor laws and contract provisions pertaining to minors are reviewed.

Actors' Equity

Although Actors' Equity (the union for actors working in the theater) oversees the contracts of many children working in shows like *Miss Saigon* and *The Sound of Music,* not only in New York City, but in cities all over the country, the union has no provisions in their contracts for young performers.

They do, however offer seminars on topics such as: *Touring and the Family; Interaction with Agents, Managers and Financial Advisors; Careers Behind the Scenes* and *The Transition from Child to Adult Performer.*

Managers

There's a full treatment of the pros and cons of having managers in Chapter 12. Although I'm not a proponent of managers in general, the one area where I feel they do some real good can be with children.

If you are a child or the parent of a child entering the business, it's likely you could use some guidance concerning pictures, resumes, proper training and set behavior. Managers also have a pulse on the agents in the area, know the demands of the marketplace and can arrange meetings with various agents and oversee those relationships. It's not necessary to have a manager, but it can save you time. If your child is marketable, you can easily act as his/her manager. Just send good snapshots to a children's agent along with a letter telling them about the child. If they feel the child can work, most will be happy to educate you.

Unlike agents, managers are not licensed or franchised, nor do they have any rules governing them. There are some really good managers and some really bad ones. Most managers charge 15% commission, on top of the 10% charged by agents.

A good manager is someone who also coaches the kids, goes with them on the interviews and helps them get the job, nurtures them and helps choose appropriate classes.

Set Behavior

If your child does work in the business, it is your responsibility to make sure the child does not dominate the set. Neither the director, the assistant director, nor the other actors are responsible for parenting your child. If your child acts like a child and is obnoxious from time to time, it is not the responsibility of the creative staff to keep him in line. You might feel that if the director or the assistant director tells your child, he might be more likely to respond. Don't give up your place with your child. It's up to you to make sure he behaves not only professionally, but as a happy addition to the set.

If your child is going to be on the set, he should be on time, attentive, respectful and as focused as possible. (This is why I don't think it's a good idea to make a child conform this much until he is an adult.) He is being paid as an adult and it is extremely rude and unfair to the adults on the set (who are trying to be accommodating, but also have their own jobs to attend to) when he is allowed to absorb everyone else's time and energy.

Jodi Foster, Elizabeth Taylor, Shirley Temple and Ron Howard are the only mega-famous child stars I can think of who seemed to have made it to adulthood in tact. Few are able to balance showbiz success with a successful adulthood beyond the business.

Ron Howard's father says that one reason Ron never lost his perspective was that Mr. and Mrs. Howard (both actors) made sure that they never used Ron's money to upgrade their standard of living. As long as they were still supporting Ron and the family, they retained their parental position in the family and Ron was able to stay a little boy.

It's pretty hard to come down hard on someone who is paying your rent or who has enough money in his bank account to leave at the first cross word.

Obviously money is the lure that seduces parents to not only give up their own free time, but their kid's childhood as well.

Kids/Money

So, after all the classes, coaching, auditioning and missing baseball games and Brownie meetings, what are the possible financial rewards?

✦ *"On most shows, kids start around $5,000 an episode," says one executive. "They tend to have built-in raises [like adult actors] that are 5% or, if they're lucky, 10% per year. They sign seven year contracts; virtually no one will hire a performer without that. With*

*break-out characters, I'd say renegotiation is the norm by the third
or fourth year on a successful show. But you only give more money in
return for something else."*
  Age of Innocence?
  Stephen Galloway
  Hollywood Reporter Showbiz Kids Special Issue
  November 1, 1994

Before you put those numbers into your calculator,
understand that even though there are usually 22 shows
in a season, not all performers on a show are signed for
all shows. A usual contract can call for 7 of 13 shows or
10 of 13. That formula translates to 12 of 22 and so on.

The contract that confines the actor does not bind
the producer. Every year when/if the show is picked up,
management has the right not to exercise the option on
the actor's services. No such alternative exists for the
actor.

Minorities/Girls/Boys

Just as in the adult world, there are more jobs for
little white boys than for anyone else. In the *Hollywood
Reporters' Special Showbiz Kids Issue,* casting directors Jane
Jenkins and Janet Hirshenson, who have cast youngsters
in *Mrs. Doubtfire, My Life, Jurassic Park, Dennis the Menace*
and many other films, were interviewed concerning the
discrepancy in the numbers of parts for girls and boys.

✦   *I think it's largely a similar situation for little-girl actresses
as it is for big-girl actresses. The majority of the scripts that are
written are written by men and they write about their own
childhoods. And the majority of men are directors and producers,
and so they pick material that has some personal meaning to them.
There are just very few projects that really feature strong women,
although there are a few more than there used to be.*

Casting a Spell
Stephen Galloway
The Hollywood Reporter Showbiz Kids Special Issue
November 1, 1994

Kim Fields played Tootie on NBC's hit sitcom, *Facts of Life*, the only black actress in an all white show. She also starred on Fox's *Living Single*. She was asked if it was tough overcoming the obstacles of being a black woman:

✦ *I didn't look at them as obstacles, just non-changing facts. My sex wasn't changing, my race wasn't changing. So it just became a part of the package.*
Growing Up, Living Single
Michael Arkush
Los Angeles Times
December 24, 1994

We all have to find a way to think positively about unchanging facts. One of those rare kid actors who has managed to translate her earlier success into adult employment, Kim has worked to expand herself. She earned a degree in telecommunications from Pepperdine University and is not only directing for the theater, but has produced her own 35-minute short film. She talked candidly about her own rough times:

✦ *Just knowing I had something to fall back on helped. The work ethic didn't just disintegrate. The doubts fueled positive motivation that I needed to learn how to do something else, so I wouldn't be sitting around waiting for my agent to call. I would have gone crazy sitting in my apartment doing that. I learned how to direct and produce. I got my education, so that validates me.*
Growing Up, Living Single
Michael Arkush
Los Angeles Times
December 24, 1994

Gullible Parents

In every business, there are unscrupulous characters seeking to separate the vulnerable from their money. No one can guarantee your child an audition, a job or a career. All an agent can do is promise to introduce your child to the buyers. Some agents have more ability to do that than others.

The agreement agents made with Screen Actors Guild in order to obtain a franchise forbids agents from engaging in any kind of commerce with their clients other than seeking acting employment.

Most agents have a handout list of photographers that some of their clients use, but if your agent insists you use his photographer and/or sells you acting lessons, this is in violation of his agreement with the guild.

If you are encouraged by an agent or a manager to pay to see them, to pay to be listed with them, to use their photographer or to pay them for acting lessons, beware.

✦ *Two operators of a Beverly Hills talent agency who claimed they could turn children into actors and models have been ordered to spend 30 days in jail for making false promises to parents, who sometimes paid thousands of dollars up-front.*

"Most of the parents had been enticed by telemarketer to bring their children to auditions sponsored by West Coast Talent," Lambert said.

"After the auditions," he said, "the agency pressured clients to pay fees for acting classes, photo portfolios and the chance to audition in front of casting directors."

Sandy Bosnich, one of the original claimants, said she paid $6,000 to West Coast Talent after she was told her three daughters all had the potential for success in commercials. She said the company provided photographs and acting classes but never fulfilled the promise of work. Lambert said the families never got such auditions.

2 Talent Agency Operators Given 30-Day Jail Terms
Kurt Streeter
The Los Angeles Times
January 30, 1999

A Final Word to Parents

Think carefully before exposing yourself or your child to showbiz. It's a heartbreaker for adults and even harder for people who have not yet reached their own personhood, and therefore cannot really make an educated decision.

Wrap Up

✓ your kid only has one shot at being a kid
✓ your child is paid as an adult, make sure he behaves as one
✓ write for Screen Actors Guild's free pamphlet: *Young Performers Handbook*
✓ know the Child Labor Laws of your state
✓ make your own guidelines if your state has no code or if it doesn't go as far as you think it should
✓ don't live on your child's money
✓ don't be gullible

10 Actually Pursuing Work

The best way to look for work is to work. Since you can't be in the union until you get a job, but you can't have a job until you are in the union, how are you going to scale the castle walls?

Actually, you can find work, just not union work. You want to join the union and become a professional actor as soon as possible, I know, but have patience; it's not wise to join the union until you have amassed a few impressive credits and in LA/NY at least, have some film to show. At that point, when you are actually marketable, *then* it's time to join the union. There's more on union joining or not in Chapter 13.

Pictures and Resumes

No matter what market you are in, you are going to have to come up with pictures and resumes. You will need pictures for the newspapers, casting directors and producers as well as to introduce yourself to the various organizations in your community.

Look at other actors' pictures to see what appeals to you when selecting a photographer. Look at all the other pictures that have ever been taken of you, including snapshots. Isolate what is most interesting about the best ones. If you feel you can't analyze them appropriately, consider taking a photography or art class to develop a more discerning eye.

One of my favorite New York photographers, Van Williams, knows how anxious actors can get about having their pictures made, so he encourages them to go through a warmup routine of exercises to relax themselves. I think stretching as you finish putting on your wardrobe is a good idea. If you can make time to meditate a few minutes before your pictures, that would also be a help.

The most important aspect of any photo is that it look exactly like you. It's self defeating to choose a photographer who takes glamour photos if you are a regular person. If a casting director calls you in expecting to see Cindy Crawford and you are Kathy Najimy, he is not going to be pleased. Forget about trying to change people's minds, casting directors are busy. They have their orders from on high and they are trying to fill them.

Analyze every picture you see. Look at the pictures your friends are using, but don't let those pictures make your decisions; just use them for research. Make up your own mind. When I am choosing my own pictures from a contact sheet, I try to decide which of the images is the person I would want to approach and speak to at a party. Also check to make sure all parts of the picture are sharp and clear and that the top of your head is not cut off. These things seem elemental, but you would be surprised what some photographers get away with when actors are just concentrating on their faces.

If you have an agent, it is always wise to get his input regarding these decisions since he will be selling you via the pictures. He will have concrete ideas about what is best. Learn more by asking him how he made his choices.

It's usually not a good idea to let photographers choose. Their criteria for a good picture is not yours. They are not necessarily in a position to know what is the best representation of you relative to selling yourself as an actor.

A couple of suggestions for those of you who may live in a town where duplicating pictures is frightfully expensive. Duplicate Photos in Los Angeles does a great deal of its business via mail order. They do a good job of mass producing pictures and giving you a fair price at the same time. You can check out information on them at their website: http://www.duplicate.com or via phone: 323-466-7544/818-760-4193.

At a recent trade show for actors, I picked up some impressive samples from Modern Postcard. They are located in Carlsbad, California and specialize in color

Mary Smith\555-4489
5' 4", 115 lbs, blonde hair, blue eyes

Theater

Romeo and Juliet . . . . name of theater
Sweet Bird of Youth . . . . name of theater

Film

Shakespeare in Love . . . . name of director
You've Got Mail . . . . name of director

Television

ER . . . . name of director
Spin City . . . . name of director

Commercials

First National Bank, Local Gas Company, Local
Newspaper, etc.

Training

acting . . . . teacher
singing . . . . teacher
dance . . . . teacher

skills: Speak Spanish fluently, horseback riding,
gymnastics, ballroom dancing, commercial
driving license, etc.

postcards. Modern Postcard offers two sizes of cards. Standard size is 4 1/4 by 6 inches. Deluxe size is 6 by 8 ½ inches. Their prices are terrific @ 500 for $95 plus postage. Phone 800-959-8365 for information or check their website: http://www.modernpostcard.com

Wardrobe

Consider the purpose of the photos when you are choosing wardrobe. Commercial casting directors usually like to see you in plaid shirts/blouses and sweaters. Theatrical pictures need to sell you in a more formal way. Musical performers require a trendier approach. Study CD covers for ideas. Make sure your photo fulfills the appropriate criteria.

In general, buyers are interested in a full-front representation of you. No hands up to the face; it's too distracting. Choose clothing that is relatively plain. You're not selling clothes, you want them looking at you. Unless you are shooting color, black and white clothing is usually not a good choice because the severe contrast is not flattering. Red, green and other medium tones usually photograph more appealingly.

Your resume should be attached to your 8x10 glossy print. You can have your picture printed with or without a white border (some agents prefer the picture without border, but it is usually more expensive). The resume should be stapled to the back so that as you turn the picture over, you see the resume as though it were printed on the back side of the photo.

The buyers see hundreds of resumes every day. Yours should be simple and easy to read. Not only is it not necessary to have millions of jobs listed, but when prospective employers see too much writing, their eyes will glaze over and they won't read anything. Choose the most impressive credits and list them.

There is a prototype on the following page for you to use as a guide for form. Lead with your strong suit. If you have done more commercials than anything else, list that as your first category; if you are a singer, list music.

You may live in a market where theater credits are taken very seriously. If so, even though you may have done more commercials, lead with theater if you have anything credible to report.

Adapt this prototype to meet your needs. If all you have done is college theater, list it. That is more than someone else has done and it will give the buyer an idea of what you can do. If you have nothing to put on your resume, list your training and a physical description.

If you do book reviews, list places where you have done them. If you sing, list where. Note that you were master of ceremonies for your town Pioneer Day Celebration. Whatever. As you have more important credits, drop the less impressive ones.

My own opinion is not to put your union affiliation (Screen Actors Guild, Actor's Equity Association, American Federation of Television and Radio Artists) on the resume. Writing down that you are a member of the union makes me think you just got accepted into the union and/or have nothing else to write on the resume.

The most important thing on your resume is that your name and contact number be prominently displayed. If you have an agent, use his phone number instead of yours. If you don't have an agent, list an answering service or phone mail. It's safer and more professional not to list your personal number for business phone calls.

No matter what, have call waiting. You don't want your agent to have difficulty reaching you. Have a reliable answering service or answering machine. Some paranoid souls have both for that off-day when the phone is out of order.

Taking Care of Business

Keep a Rolodex of business contacts. In New York and Los Angeles, this might mean casting directors, producers, directors, agents, etc. In a smaller town, it might mean ad agencies, radio personnel, newspaper people; whoever buys talent in your marketplace.

Note every contact: when you met, spoke and/or wrote, what the contact was about, results, etc. Record the person's physical description and where he sits in his office so you will be sure to recognize him next time. Note something the two of you talked about as well as any personal information you might have on him.

Go through your Rolodex at least once a week to see who you need to call or write a note to. Keep in touch even if there isn't something specific to talk about. Remember those AT&T commercials: you never know what will come out of a phone call.

It's not easy to do these things. It takes energy and sometimes it's scary. Even though it may appear fruitless, it isn't. All the energy you put out will come back, maybe not today or tomorrow, but it will come back. Practice using your imagination, creativity and courage every day. It will get easier. After all, these people are your business partners; you all need each other.

Respond to Good Work

Everybody likes to know their work has been recognized. Call or write a note to a casting director that you have worked with and tell her what a good job she did on a specific project. Directors and producers you have worked with will also appreciate recognition.

Anne Archer tells a wonderful story about working with Glenn Close. As the star of their film, *Fatal Attraction,* Glenn saw the first rough cut. She immediately sat down and wrote a detailed letter to Anne citing her best moments, scene by scene. Could you ever forget that kind of generosity?

Years ago, I was fortunate to be cast in the film, *A Touch of Class.* By the time I joined the cast in Spain, they had already bonded in London with a month's prior shooting. The second night, we all sat in a crowded hotel dining room looking at dailies. It was uncomfortable and close, but in the middle of the screening, someone crawled all the way across the dark room, through a tangle of chairs and legs and tapped me on the knee. It was George Segal telling me he thought my work was good. I'll never forget how that made me feel.

Scratching Isn't All Bad

You aren't going to believe me, but I have to say it anyway: early success can be the kiss of death. With success comes visibility and judgement. Everyone waits to see if you are a flash in the pan and can live up to your early promise. You no longer have the luxury of anonymity in which to refine your art; therefore, it's much more expensive and scary to change anything.

What if no one likes your work when you change directions? So now, not only are you afraid to experiment, but you may get an unrealistic picture of the business. Seem unlikely? Let's assume you get to Los Angeles and because you are cute and adorable and young and new, you luck into a large or small part on a television series. Whether it runs two years or ten, the following things have happened: you've made more money than ever before and probably adjusted your lifestyle accordingly. You are recognizable or semi-recognizable (depending on the status of the show). Production assistants call you Miss or Mr. and get chairs and food for you. Producers and directors treat you with great respect and listen intently to your ideas and complaints (whether or not they act on them).

Regardless of the tenure of the show, you have had one job and played one part. Unless you've gotten a TV movie during your hiatus (and only really visible players on top ten rated shows usually have that option) or scored a play during that same time span, you have not grown as an actor at all. But while you were regularly employed, you never noticed and no one seemed to care. You may be surprised and hurt when the show is over when you have to fetch your own coffee and no one

wants to know you. You are now considered over
exposed and have to sit out a few years while the public
stops identifying you as that character.

Hector Elizondo spoke of other hazards:

✦ *The danger, of course, is in insulating yourself, especially if
you become popular. You lose sight of the rest of the world. Luckily
all this commercial attention has happened at this time of my life,
[Hector struggled for years before he became visible] because I've
seen what it does to folks who are not ready for it at a very early
age. And it's devastating because you have a tendency to slip into
the illusory world of believing that you are important, and believing
that what you are doing is valuable and terrific.*

*The biggest danger is compromising your standards of
work. Because everyone is patting you on the back, you lose sight of
your limitations, your objectives, your growth — suddenly showing
up is enough.*

*The problem is that if you're too young and it happens too
soon, you get buried under the illusion of it.*

From Pretty Woman to Plenty Busy
Elias Stimac
Drama-Logue
Sept. 19-26, 1991

Harrison Ford is an actor who has managed to
stay grounded in spite of great success:

✦ *Unlike a lot of actors, Ford doesn't ever refer to himself as
an artist, preferring to engage in a rear-guard campaign of
reductionism, describing himself variously as a "worker in a service
industry" and an "assistant storyteller." He deflects all attempts to
correlate the success of his films with any underlying personal
affection that audiences might feel for him.*

*"I think that that's a result of a relationship not to who I
am, but a degree of satisfaction with the product that I am part of,"
he says, sounding strangely like a vacuum cleaner salesman. "I
make audience movies. I work for them, and I think they have a
sense that I am a loyal, and to whatever degree, capable employee of
theirs."*

Danger is his Business

Bruce Newman
The Los Angeles Times/Calendar
August 14, 1994

Process Process Process

As long as you don't start taking yourself too seriously (whether you are currently working or out of work), you will be fine. It is imperative that you are able to conceptualize the ups and downs as part of the process. A job is just a job, some are more visible, some are more lucrative, and though you may be able to figure out a way to capitalize on it, the job will be still over. Make sure you have a life to return to when you're no longer in fashion.

In the 70s, Michael Douglas was a success on the hit television series, *The Streets of San Francisco*. Many actors might have banked that money, considered themselves a success and waited out the overexposure and lack of work that frequently comes after such high visibility and hoped for the best.

But Michael wanted a film career and when no one appeared to be interested, Michael, being the entrepreneurial person that he is, figured out a way to become a force in the business. Fourteen years earlier, his father had bought the rights to a property in which he hoped to star. Michael rescued the orphaned material and found a way to make *One Flew Over the Cuckoo's Nest* a successful Academy Award winning film.

As a successful producer, Michael had the attention of the film community, but still no one came forward with interesting acting offers, so Michael produced and starred in the huge hit, *Romancing the Stone*. Now, of course, he does not have to produce his own projects in order to be offered meaty parts.

It's true he had a rich, powerful and successful father and because of his background, he obviously had a close-up view of how business was conducted in the film community. It's also true that not all star off-spring manage to translate this largesse into brilliant careers. The bottom line is that Michael Douglas went in and created his own professional life.

Actress Illeana Douglas (no relation as far as I know) had a breakthrough experience in the film, *Cafe Fear*. The following year, she shared a page in *Film Comment* with John Leguizamo, Brad Pitt and Samuel L. Jackson as New Faces of the Year. But, as Douglas wrote in *Premiere Magazine*, just as Brad Pitt was signing at CAA, she was at another audition.

Taking things into her own hands, she took the money she had made from the movie, *Alive*, and decided to produce her own movie:

✦ ... *Shooting a movie in two days has its drawbacks. While the actresses showed up for day two the crew did not. But the greatest thing about such disasters is that there's no turning back. "In the end, I was able to accomplish two things: use personal material (making fun of women as victims — mainly myself) and do in ten minutes what most major studios can't do in two hours — give 30 women a job. Much to my surprise,* The Perfect Woman *took on a life of its own. It traveled the festival circuit (including Sundance, Aspen and Edinburgh) and closed the New York Film Festival, sharing the bill with* The Piano. *It played on* Bravo *and was picked up by Miramar to be distributed with* Camilla."

So an actress who just wanted to work ended up being a director to find work for herself.

"... *Gus Van Sant gave me a picture he had painted. The inscription on the back reads, 'Be your own flying saucer...rescue yourself.' And you can do that anywhere."*

Perfect Casting: Okay, So There Are No Good
Roles for Women. I Could Sit Around and Complain
— or I Could Do Something About It
Illeana Douglas
Premiere Magazine
Special Issue 1994

In the old studio days, it was possible to be discovered. Potential was recognized, signed, and groomed for stardom. Today actors who want to work must recognize their own potential, nurture it, watch it blossom and learn to sell it themselves.

It Isn't Easy Being Green

After you learn to be pushy, learn to be patient. In the beginning, you are not going to work for two or three years, maybe more. Prepare for that. It's part of the process. It takes time not only to tune your instrument and perfect your craft, but to understand the mores of Hollywood.

In speaking about indulging in an openly gay love affair with her partner, Ellen DeGeneres, Anne Heche says she is still green in some areas of her life

✦ *Unfortunately, we thought the world was bigger than that, that Hollywood was bigger than that. We were naive and we're reminded of that all the time.*
    We Were Naive
    Hilary de Vries
    The Los Angeles Times Magazine
    November 29, 1998

The day after the article appeared, Heche's partner, DeGeneres made a dramatic announcement:

✦ *The former star of ABC's* Ellen — *the first sitcom with a gay lead character whose coming out made television history —* told The Times *that she and partner Anne Heche, who co-stars in the remake of* Psycho, "want to take at least a year off. We've quit our agents, let go of our publicist, we're selling our house and leaving town," DeGeneres said.
    "...what we've found is that this is a very hard town to be truthful in."
    DeGeneres Says She and Heche Are Quitting Hollywood
    Hilary de Vries
    The Los Angeles Times
    December 1, 1998

Both DeGeneres and Heche are extremely talented and likeable performers and they will surely be back, but their careers have both suffered from their respective learning curves regarding Hollywood and the many factors that govern moving forward in the business. It takes a long time to work your way into the system. And even then, doors can close quickly.

Creating Your Own System

When people talk about networking, they don't really mean you should try to become friends with Jeff Sagansky (DreamWorks); they mean you should be a real friend to your peers. These are the stars, producers, writers and directors of tomorrow. They will rise to the top in the same time frame as you and you all can help each other. You know each other's foibles and have already learned to live with them. There is nothing sweeter than working with your friends.

Go Out There and Get Your Fifty Nos

There seems to be a certain no to yes ratio. Some actors say they get ten nos to every yes they receive. There are some periods of one's career when it certainly seems like you need fifty nos to get one yes. It's part of the business. That being the case, you may as well get started. The only problem is, every time you get a yes, there will still be fifty more nos lined up there someplace in your career waiting for you.

My brother is a salesman who seemingly thrives on abuse. Whenever a prospective customer keeps him waiting or treats him rudely, Jim just smiles to himself. He believes that people basically do feel guilty about bad behavior and he makes sure he capitalizes on that guilt by getting an even bigger order.

Wherever you live, uncovering showbiz related work requires answering a few questions:

- Who in the marketplace employs actors?
- How can I become employed?
- What jobs other than straight acting are suitable to actors?

If you are in New York or Los Angeles, it is easy to figure out that the major areas of employment are theater, film, television and commercials. Yet even there, the life of an actor is not all Macbeth and Excedrin commercials. As a matter of fact, most of it isn't.

In the primary entertainment centers, actors are spokespersons for conventions and do voice overs for radio and television commercials. They supply American dialogue for foreign films and appear in front of Madison Square Garden wearing sandwich boards and handing out buttons. They work industrial shows and do weird commercials on *Saturday Night Live, The Tonight Show* and *Late Night with David Letterman.* They spend a lot of money sending out pictures and resumes. They spend hours waiting in line for open calls for parts that have probably already been cast. Not only that, most of them feel grateful for any opportunity to get up in public to perform, to add to their resume and mostly to make money in anything related to the business.

If there are no opportunities for straight acting in plays, etc., isolate the kind of situation that will give you a chance to make a living within the atmosphere of show business. Perhaps you can be the film critic on local radio or create an innovative cooking show with public access as your entree into television.

When I started in the business in Dallas, one of the important jobs for local actors was the annual Automobile Show. If you were pretty/ handsome enough, you might be employed to stand by the car all day in evening attire looking for all the world like a very expensive accessory. If you were p/h and could also talk, you might be the spokesperson who would speak while another p/h illustrated features of the car.

You can do anything if you have nerve. One summer after the regular season was over at the Margo

Jones Theater, where I was lucky enough to apprentice, I wondered: *What is it like to go into an agent's office in Dallas, Texas?*

This was in the '50s and Dallas was not the entertainment center it is has become today. I looked in the phone book and found that, indeed, Dallas did have an agency. It was called The Molly O'Day Agency. I showed up without an appointment and announced that I was a singer. Coached by Betty Grable movies, I was expecting to be shown the door. The conversation went something like this:

> Molly: *Do you have an accompanist?*
> Me: *No.*
> Molly: *Well then, do you have any music?*
> Me: *No.*
> Molly: *Wait here.*

Miss O'Day went down the hall and reappeared with an accordion player. I had sung twice in the variety show in college and knew my key for a couple of songs. After a couple of choruses of *I'm Looking Over a Four Leaf Clover* and *It Had to be You*, the accordion player left and I was offered a job singing in the officer's club of a nearby Air Force base. My natural chutzpah got me that far, but my Catholic school training prevailed and I was unable to actually look at my audience, so my Air Force singing career was pretty short.

I also worked conventions. For one of them, I was dressed as a woman from space who did a voiceless skit. The audience had to pick up earphones to hear what we were mouthing, but they could never figure how our mouths matched what was coming out of the earphones. They didn't know we had little earphones under the space caps. This job entailed being able to move well, learn dialogue and lip sync.

I had a lucrative recurring job with Polaroid requiring that I pose with and take pictures of all the guests at a particular trade show. They trained me to set up the lights for the camera, take test pictures and deal with all the equipment and the guests.

I also taught acting at my high school alma mater, started a children's theater and wrote my own material. I worked out an arrangement with my local shopping center to use their community room at the bank for free in return for providing holiday themed entertainment on special occasions. I wrote and produced short plays and the shopping center provided space, prizes or handouts and publicity for the event.

My students had the chance to perform for more than their parents and friends. The event was successful for both merchants and students and I was making my first money in show business. It was not an extravagant amount of money, but when you start any business, you have to be prepared for meager earnings the first few years.

Work Begets Work

An actress friend started in an even smaller market: Alice, Texas. She found a way to make money from her theater degree by making book reviews her specialty. Rosemary read the latest best seller, condensed the story and then contacted the ladies' clubs and service organizations and offered her services. Clubs of this type are always looking for luncheon activities. She would tailor her review to the event, tell a couple of jokes and charge $50 or whatever the traffic would bear.

As in all other phases of this business, work begets work. She did a good job and other jobs appeared. She became the star of her town. It wasn't enough to keep her in caviar, but a little here and a little there all added up.

I met her after she had moved to Dallas and found herself intimidated by what seemed to her to be a really big city. Since I was beginning what turned out to be six years of pregnancy, I willed her all my old jobs. She was smart and parlayed them into even more.

When the film, *Paper Moon* was shooting in

Dallas, Rosemary got a part. Besides acting whenever she gets a chance, I was not surprised to discover she now writes a column for a local newspaper and has written several books.

If you live in a small town, you might have to travel to find work. When I moved to Oklahoma, the first thing I did was check out advertising agencies in the phone book in nearby Oklahoma City.

I asked if they produced television commercials and about the procedure to become involved. Since I had done commercials in Dallas, those credits added to my credibility. My husband was a grad student at the University nearby, so I called their motion picture department and subsequently worked on educational films. Money for me and film for my future.

Every working actor has a pocketful of similar stories. Successful actors call and ask where the jobs are. You need to have the imagination and determination to call everybody.

Australian actress, Toni Collette, who starred in *Muriel's Wedding*, hit the ground running when she got out of college:

✦   *Raised in Melbourne, where she still lives, she studied art, drama and dance in college before settling on acting.*

"The first year I came out of college," she says, "I wrote three plays that were performed in various fringe festivals and alternative spaces. I was working for my friends, and my friends were working for me."

Muriel's Wedding *Brings Bliss to Two Young Actresses*
Manohla Dargis
The New York Times
April 16, 1995

Unemployed/Not Working

There is a real difference between being an unemployed actor and not working. Not working implies that you usually do. But once identified as unemployed, casting directors don't really want to know you. What a casting director wants, more than anything, is to think he has discovered a terrific actor with impressive credits that no one knows anything about. He can then uncover a fresh face who is somehow experienced without being overexposed and doesn't have a big price tag. Buying talent is just like buying a dress, everybody loves to think they're getting a bargain.

Getting Noticed

Actors have been using their creativity for centuries figuring out how to get people to notice them. Post card campaigns. Balloon deliveries. Presents. Candy. Strip-O-Grams. These ideas have been used on agents so many times that they engender little more than a smile or a shake of the head coupled with eyes rolled heavenward.

I know an actor who did something extremely clever, only to have his agent (who had supported his idea initially) turn on him when the casting directors became offended.

The actor invested a lot of money, time and imagination creating a milk carton filled with candy which he had delivered to the casting directors. The gimmick was that his picture was on all the milk cartons. Under it was written the word *missing*. The actor had been out of work for some length of time and was looking for a way to get himself back before the buyers. The milk carton also listed his description, credits and agent's phone number.

As it turned out, some of the casting directors became offended with the milk carton idea. They felt that the whole idea of missing children and milk cartons was too important to be joked about. Well, of course, they're right. The actor had been so caught up in marketing, that he had not taken in the whole picture.

Call yourself to the casting director's attention without seeming desperate and/or unemployed. Actors wring their hands and say:

How?

By doing good work. If you have to produce it yourself, do it. If you are good, the material is right and you are ready, agents and casting directors will find you. In the meantime, you are your own agent. Look at all casting notices. Be in plays. Get up in front of people at every opportunity. This is part of your training and part of your life. People don't become actors to be shrinking violets.

The other part of this equation (which I cannot stress too strongly) is that one must get out of the business of being chosen and into the business of acting. That means that it may be even more valuable to mount your own vehicle and act in it than for somebody else to hire you.

Gretchen Cryer and Nancy Ford, writers and composers of *I'm Getting My Act Together and Taking It on the Road*, say they only began being taken seriously when they began to produce their own material. Earlier productions had been noticed, but when they put their money on the table, they became part of the system in New York theater.

I know how easy it is to be caught up in the madness of *I am only valid if somebody else chooses me*, but if you indulge that kind of thinking, your life will be a nightmare. If you are constantly focused on being chosen, you can never become a valid person: you will always be second guessing what someone else might want. Do they want me to be funnier here? uglier? prettier? They don't know. When you go shopping you don't always know exactly what you want, but when your eye catches something, you know that was lingering in your subconscious the whole time: *Yes, this is what I want, I didn't even know it existed, but I must have it.*

Bob King/Saxophone

Bob King is an ingenious actor who started his

showbiz career as a young musician, playing the saxophone. The way musicians got jobs at that time, was to go to the hiring hall and wait to be called. Someone who needed a piano player would come in, stand up and yell out: *John Smith — piano* and John would get up and walk out with his new employer. When Bob first came to the hall, he sized up the situation and instead of just sitting there waiting to be called, he walked in, cupped his hands and called out: *Bob King — saxophone* and then pretended to see someone across the room and walked out. After several weeks of that, one day a prospective employer asked who he was, Bob answered: *I'm Bob King, I play saxophone* and the man replied, *Oh yeah, I've heard of you. Come on!*

This is absolutely one of the best stories about getting work I ever heard, topped only by a later story of Bob's. After his career as a musician, Bob became very popular in commercials. A casting director ran into him one day and said, *Oh, Bob. You are becoming the George Jenkins of commercials.* Bob didn't know what that meant, so he went to George Jenkins and asked. George replied, *Oh, that means you are getting ready to be overexposed. You'd better develop a voice-over career or something fast. I got overexposed and couldn't get an on-camera job for two years.*

Like most of us in those days, Bob worked through many different agents for commercials and often had several auditions in a single day, so the next time an agent called him, he put a new plan into action. When an agent said, *Be at Y&R at 10 AM for Lipton's Tea,* Bob said, *Oh, could it be at 11:15? I have a voice-over booking.* He continued to change every single appointment he got for the next two weeks until finally an agent said, *Well, who in the hell is getting you all this voice work?* Ever shrewd Bob answered sweetly: *Not you,* and a big voice-over career was born.

Casting Directors

Most beginning (and even experienced actors) wouldn't dream of trying to call on a casting director personally, but casting directors are not as inaccessible as your fantasies might lead you to believe. I know an actor who had been quite successful in commercials in New York. For some reason (he now doesn't know why either), he had the idea that when he moved to Los Angeles, agents would be waiting for him with open arms. Of course, anyone who has spent any time in Los Angeles (or New York) will be happy to tell you that being a commercial actor or even a soap actor doesn't mean much to film and television people. It is a whole different part of the business.

My friend, a business-oriented and determined type, decided to do for himself what agents would not. He would get himself in to see the casting directors. He made a list and every day he targeted five casting directors to call. He sent a picture and resume. When he made the follow-up call, he always found out to whom he was speaking and noted the name and date.

Invariably, the casting director (or assistant) would say he was not seeing anyone right now. My friend then asked when he would be seeing people again. If the casting director said three weeks, the actor would note the date and call in three weeks. This went on until he actually got an appointment.

His feeling was that people begin to feel guilty after a while, and will finally see you just because they can't handle saying *no* again. He got a lot of jobs that way and eventually landed an agent.

So, if a casting director tells you to call back in three weeks, do so. Always call the person by name: *Hi, Mary? This is Kelly Smith again. How are you? What did you think about the Academy Awards (Dodgers, earthquake, etc.)? I was just wondering if you have any time to see me tomorrow, I'm going to be over in that direction anyway.*

Elizabeth Pena, who starred in *Batteries Not*

Included, La Bamba and *Jacob's Ladder,* got her first job in a feature by being relentless.

After several fruitless months in Los Angeles, she read of the then upcoming feature *Down and Out In Beverly Hills* directed by Paul Mazursky, who liked Latins. Undeterred by the fact that she had no agent, Pena began bombarding the film's casting director with photos, letters and resumes. She finally persuaded a studio guard to deliver a demo tape and eventually wound up with the role of the sultry maid, Carmen:

✦ *I believe you should just go for it. There's no door thick enough; if it's too thick, you blast it open. If you have to get through, you have to get through.*
    Close Ups
    Libby Slate
    Premiere Magazine
    Spring 1988

Kathy Najimy, who plays opposite Kirsti Alley in *Veronica's Closet,* had already spent time doing stand-up, improvisation and political theater when she teamed up with Mo Gaffney to create a cabaret act that ran Off-Broadway, won several Obies and was made into an HBO special. From that exposure, Kathy was cast in six movies in two years, she and Gaffney got a two-picture writing assignment with Hollywood Pictures and the CBS development deal that put her into *Veronica's Closet.*

Gary Sinese is another actor who took matters into his own hands:

✦ *I can honestly say that I've done everything I've wanted to do, always. Not without difficulty. But every time I wanted to do something, I just did it. From the age of 18 when I started my own theater with my friends. When I decided I wanted to act, I just bit the bullet. It's terribly difficult out here. There were plenty of times when I wasn't working.*

Gary After Gump
Virginia Campbell
Movieline
June 1995

Action breeds success; go get things, go make things happen, go do the work.

Once you become a force financially, there will be agents and managers who will want to hitch their wagons to yours and may even initiate work for you, but your vision still needs to fuel the engine.

Sharon Stone has managed her career beautifully; I love what she says about taking risks:

✦   *I think risks are terribly exciting. I'd rather lose than be timid. After all, we're just the amalgamation of the experiences we've had. If you don't take risks, eventually, you're nothing.*
          Dame Fame
          Virginia Campbell
          Movieline
          June 1994

Doing Your Own Publicity

On any given day, in any given city, where there are theatrical agents, you'll find disgruntled actors who will tell you their agents never get them any work at all. And they may be right.

I believe that the best agent in the world can't sell you if you are not a marketable product. It's still up to you to create that product and to keep making it marketable. One of the ways to do that is with publicity.

It's amazing how much publicity you can actually get for yourself. One follows the same procedure no matter where you live. Although you can just send information addressed *To the Editor*, you will have better luck if you will do a little research.

Target a periodical and read it for a bit to digest a couple of names. When you are ready to submit material, call the editorial department and ask to speak to the person at the publication that your research has uncovered as most likely to be interested in your type of information. This will usually be the entertainment or theater editor, but you might be able to slant your story toward general features if you can tie in another element. In any event, make sure you ask for and send to the appropriate person by name.

If I were publicizing this book, I might call the entertainment editor or the books editor. If I slanted the story to include not only the information available in the book, but how I happened to write it in the first place and how this is my twentieth successful book, then the story would appeal to a larger audience.

If you are appearing in a play, you can send a blurb when you are cast and later, when you are opening, send another. If anything interesting or funny happened during rehearsal, you might get a few lines recounting the incident. Send in the information; they may have some space to fill that day.

Call and attempt to speak to the writer before you send material and then follow-up to see that your information arrived. On the first call, say something like, *Hello, Jane Smith? This is Laura Adams, I saw your piece on* Performing Pigs *and really thought it was funny. I cut it out and sent it to my mother (chit-chat/ chit-chat). The reason I'm calling is that I'm producing a play and I have an idea about it that I thought might interest you. Since it's turned out that everyone in the cast was in the first grade together* (or whatever else you can dream up that might be unusual or interesting and make a news story) *I thought this might make a nice feature. May I send you some information?*

She'll either say no (in which case you have saved postage and can now call up another newspaper or dream up another hook) or she'll say, yes. If she does agree to your plan, verify the exact address and tell her you'll call in a couple of days to make sure she received your packet. Then make sure you do so.

I called *The Los Angeles Times* and *Daily Variety* in Los Angeles asking general questions regarding whether one needed a publicist in order to get coverage. I asked if actors were looked down upon if they were calling for themselves. On the contrary, the editors informed me, they would prefer to talk directly to the actor. Perhaps more to a celebrity than you or me, but they did say they would, so put them to the test. If you have something truly newsworthy or funny, they will be thrilled to have it.

If you are trying to get material in a special column, call the columnist, introduce yourself and ask if he accepts material directly from actors. If he does, ask if you might send something. Drop it by personally if possible. If you don't get to see him, follow up with a phone call to make sure he got the material and thank him for his help. Be careful with his time, but take the time to be personal.

Following up takes more time and energy, but you get out what you put in. If you take the easiest route, your rewards will invariably not be as great.

In all cases, take the time to make a professional looking presentation of your material and slant the material in a unique manner. Make sure the story is typed, double-spaced and includes a contact name, address and phone number. In a small town, it's a little simpler to get space and maybe, a picture.

Television and radio are not that difficult, if you can think of an angle. The media has space and time to fill every day, so if you can make your project visually interesting and unique, you'll not only meet with success, but they'll soon be happy to hear from you. If you are just appearing in a play, that is probably not newsworthy, but if the play deals with some relevant topic or if you researched it in an interesting way, people will find it entertaining.

If you are directing or producing a play, consider dedicating the proceeds from one performance to a local charity. That way you and the charity both benefit from the publicity. Arrange a contest within the theme of the play. Have a look-alike contest. There are all sorts of ways to get the media interested, particularly in a small town. Imagine each program you are contacting as if it were your own. If you were the host of that show, what would appeal to you? Various radio stations in Los Angeles give away theater tickets provided by producers who give the tickets in exchange for the publicity. Become aware of what's going on in the media in your area and some way of fitting in will occur to you.

Fans

No matter where you live, you will begin to collect some fans along the way. Don't discount them. Fans are a symbol of your growing visibility. When I was in high school, it meant so much to me when actors answered my letters giving me advice that I make it a point to respond to fans asking for guidance at: http://hollywoodnet.com/hn/acting/insider/drawer13.html
I had a bad experience helping a young actor recently, so I'm more cautious with one-on-one meetings now. I'm afraid I'm no longer as trusting as I used to be, so I apologize if I'm harder to get in touch with.
Many actors have a mailing list and send post-cards to fans when they are in something. If you can get someone interested enough to be your fan club president, they can do those things for you. If you are ever involved in an endeavor which needs support from the public to prove to your employer it is important to keep hiring you, your fans are there to take on the challenge. That's how *Cagney & Lacey, Designing Women, Home Front* and innumerable other television shows have kept themselves on the air in the past.

Industry Jobs

The most successful method of entry is to get any kind of job at any studio. Many studios have temp pools of overqualified people to call when an employee is out. Your assignment could be anything from picking up an actor at the airport and delivering him to the set, to working in the mailroom, being a production assistant or driving a producer to appointments. I know of several people who worked as drivers and managed to pass their material on to staff writers who became their advocates.

There are temp agencies which specialize in providing workers for networks and studios, although Movie of the Week producer, Ken Raskoff, who entered the business through temp work as a secretary, said he got more access to creative people via a regular temp agency. There are more opportunities for showbiz related jobs in Los Angeles, but there are jobs in New York as well.

You don't get to choose where you are going to work if you go through an employment agency, of course, but you could end up working at WMA, ICM, Paradigm, CAA or any of the big agencies, production companies or networks. Any destination will be valuable.

Check the temp ads in the trades or call a studio yourself and ask if there is an in-house temporary employment pool. Many temp jobs work into regular employment if you strike the fancy of your employers and are clearly motivated.

I don't want to imply that getting a showbiz job is a piece of cake, but if you apply yourself, you can do it. No matter what city you live in, there is some kind of artistic community. Check out your local opportunities.

Internships

If you can't get an industry job, an internship is a great beginning. There is a lot of competition for the choice spots, but someone gets them so it might as well be you.

Many universities post industry internship possibilities on their bulletin boards. If your school doesn't or if you are not in school, it's still possible to track down your own internship.

A good resource is the excellent *Internships: A Directory for Career-Finders* by Sara Dulaney Gilbert, $18.95, an Arco book from Macmillan Press. The guide lists over 25,000 internship opportunities available nationwide, including part-time, full-time, paid and unpaid, summer and year-round internships in all fields. Most library reference desks either have that book or others like it.

For showbiz internships, a good place to gather information is through the Academy of Television Arts and Sciences. They sponsor an annual summer internship program.

Television Academy Internship Programs

The Academy of Television Arts & Sciences internships exist in 27 categories: Agency, Art Direction, Animation-Traditional, Animation-Non-Traditional, (computer generated), Broadcast Advertising & Casting, Promotion, Business Affairs, Development, Children's Programming/Development, Cinematography, Music, Commercials, Costume Design, Documentary/Reality Production, Editing, Entertainment News, Episodic Series, Movies for Television, Network Programming Management, Production Management, Public Relations & Publicity, Sound, Syndication/Distribution, Television Directing/Single Camera, Television Directing/Multi-Camera, Television Scriptwriting, and Videotape Post Production.

Last year, out of approximately 1,000 applicants, 28 were selected. The Princeton Review has recognized the ATAS program as one of the top ten internship programs of any kind in the United States.

If you are currently enrolled as a full-time student in a U.S. college or university (undergraduate or graduate) or you graduated after January 1, 1998, you are eligible to apply for the Summer 1999 Competition. (Taking extension courses does not make one eligible.) Foreign students are eligible if they meet the above requirements.

Most internships begin during mid to late June or early July depending on the schedule of the company which hosts the internship. Each internship ends 8 weeks after the start date. (The music category, however, starts in late July or August.) All positions are full-time. All internships are located in the Los Angeles area. Each intern receives a stipend of $2,000. Interns whose permanent residence is outside Los Angeles County will receive an additional $400 to help defray travel/housing expenses.

Flyers are mailed to Career Resource Centers and TV/Film Departments nationwide and are available by calling the Academy @ 818-754-2830 or on their website: http://internships@emmys.org.

There are no job guarantees, but interns learn how the television business works from the inside and definitely gives you a leg up.

By the time you read this, 1999 applications will have come and gone, but the website will keep you informed of the next deadline dates.

The Public Theater Internships

An opportunity to work at The New York Public Theater would be a real grounding into how things work in the New York theater. The Public offers internships in community affairs, marketing, press, play development, production and in the producer's office. A modest stipend is offered for a minimum commitment of 20 hours per week for a period of 3-6 months. Resume and cover letter should be mailed or faxed to

Alison Harper/Public Theater/NYSF
425 Lafayette Street
New York, NY 10003
212-539-8505

New Dramatists Internships

The nation's oldest non-profit workshop for playwrights, The New Dramatists say their internship program offers a unique opportunity to learn about professional, non-profit theater in New York City. It's also a prime place to meet emerging playwrights.

Full-time interns work at least 40 hours a week and are provided with a stipend of $25 (which mostly covers transportation and lunch). Part-time interns must work a minimum of 15 hours a week, and should be able to commit to a regular schedule (part-time internships are unpaid).

Interns are encouraged to participate in as many workshops and playwrighting classes as possible and to take advantage of the complimentary tickets to Broadway and Off-Broadway productions made available to the organization.

Internships are available in Stage Management, Public Relations/Special Events, Literary Management and Development/Administration. Applications are accepted year round.

New Dramatists/Internship Coordinator
424 W 44th St.
New York, NY 10036
Website: http://fargo.itp.tsoa.nyu.edu/~diana/playwrights.htm

Knowledge is Power

The more you know about the business in every area, the better equipped you are to handle it.

Any job you can get in any city that is industry-related will hold you in good stead as you progress along the route to your goals.

If you are not computer savvy, get that way. Computer skills enhance your marketability across the board and Internet access opens the door to knowledge and job opportunities.

The Hollywood Creative Directory not only publishes the most extensive guides to agents, managers and, all-round industry information, they maintain an informative *free* website that, in addition to providing the most up-to-date list of agents' names, phone numbers and addresses, also maintains a free Hollywood job board. I visited their website and found the following job division listings:

- Creative: Producers, Studios, Network Executives, Staff, Assistants, etc.
- Agents & Managers: Agents, Managers, Casting, Assistants, etc.
- Distributors: Sales, Marketing, Public Relations, Merchandising, Business Affairs, etc.
- New Media: Web Designers, Content Providers, Multimedia Publishers, etc.
- Production/Post Production, Crew, Editors, EFX, Recording Studios, Graphic Artists, Etc.
- Support: Assistants, Personal Assistants, Personal Trainers, Shoppers, etc.
- Interns: Entertainment Industry Internships
- Miscellaneous: Last but not least, everything else related to the Entertainment Industry

The address for Hollywood Creative Directory's online job board is: www.hcdonline.com.

Websites/Information

Screen Actors Guild (http://www.sag.com/), AFTRA (http://www.aftra.org/) and Actors Equity (http://www.actorsequity.org/) all have home pages, as do The Writers Guild (http://www.wga.org/index.html) and The Directors Guild (http://dga.org/). These sites provide current guild news as well as information on joining, fees and upcoming events.

Both the Writers and Directors Guild also excerpt articles from their magazines that will educate actors on a variety of subjects as well as help you begin to know the people who are working in the industry.

For instance, when I accessed the Directors Guild website, I found an interview with director, John Woo (*The Killer, Bullet in the Head, Broken Arrow* and *Hard Boiled*) that sheds light on how he casts:

✦ *Usually in an action movie, the actress only knows how to scream and yell and run scared. I liked Samantha Mathis because she looked different. I think she stands for a strong character, always independent. Not a scared girl who needs protection. I usually put the actors photos together, to see how they fit. And when I put their pictures together it looked like a golden boy [Slater] and golden girl. That's how we cast.*

The Woo Dynasty Comes to Hollywood
Ted Elrick
DGA Magazine
Nov-Dec 1995

Another site that will educate and entertain is the Internet Movie Database; http://us.imdb.com/credits, which will answer your movie questions concerning plot, characters, actors, actresses, directors, writers, etc. on probably every movie in existence.

Daily Variety (http://DailyVariety.com/) and *The Hollywood Reporter* (http://HollywoodReporter.com/) also have websites full of information.

Sherwood Oaks Experimental College

If you are in Los Angeles, I highly recommend the seminars at Sherwood Oaks Experimental College. Although they are slanted more towards writers, it's a wonderful place to not only meet folks who are going places in the business, but a chance to hear inspiring industry leaders talk. Gary Shusetts, who runs the place, always provides time at the end of the sessions for the audience and the panel members to interact.

I have been invited to chair several panels there and I'm always excited by who I meet.

I find that actors generally don't think to spend their money on these kinds of weekends, leaning more towards putting their money into acting, voice and dance lessons as well as those expensive 8x10s, however, I think choosing seminars wisely will net large rewards on down the line.

Sherwood Oaks Experimental College
7095 Hollywood Blvd.
PO Box 876
Hollywood, CA 90028
323-851-1769
E-mail:Sherwoodoaks@juno.com

The extension courses at UCLA also expose you to some good people. Check out their website: http://www.unex.ucla.edu/

Independent Features Projects

One of the most connected and effective support groups for filmmakers is Independent Features Projects. IFP's 2,000-plus members include writers, actors, grips, sound technicians and anyone else seeking involvement in independent film. Membership in IFP is a smart move for anyone in the business.

This national non-profit group sponsors seminars, classes, screenings, producer series, The Spirit Awards and an eclectic collection of industry resources. It is not necessary to be a member in order to attend events, but the monthly newsletter listing free screenings, get togethers, resources and ads from people wanting scripts is only available to members. Membership fees are $40 for students and $95 for individuals. Members have access to discounted health and production insurance.

Primarily a support and resource group for directors, IFP also gathers artists committed to originating their own work and helps others who are on that path.

Their webpage says that IFP is also for executives who want to stay on top of the indie film phenomenon. For networking, tracking projects, discovering talent, and for providing invaluable financing and co-production information, the IFP is the foremost link between the creative and business communities.
Website: http://www.ifp.org/

Independent Features Projects/West
Executive Director: Dawn Hudson
1964 Westwood Blvd. #205
Los Angeles, CA 90025
310-475-4379

Independent Features Projects/Midwest
Executive Director: Jim Vincent
676 N La Salle Dr.
Chicago, IL 60610-3784
312-587-1818

Independent Features Projects
Executive Director: Michele Byrd
104 W 29th St.
New York, NY 10001
212-465-8200

Independent Features Projects/North
Executive Director: Jane Minton-Fors
401 N 3rd St., #450
Minneapolis, MN 55401-1351
612-338-0871

Independent Features Projects/South
Executive Director: Richard Seres
PO Box 145246
Coral Gables, FL 33114
305-461-3544

Hollywood Shorts

Although Hollywood Shorts bills themselves as a resource for directors, executive director Kimberly Browning, tells me their monthly meetings frequently showcase short films directed by actors. These entrepreneurs become hyphenates in order to create work for themselves and their friends.

Created in the summer of 1998, Hollywood Shorts presents films of four to five directors and their productions teams to audiences of 150-200 people at invitation only screenings of fellow filmmakers, independent producers, reps from film and television studios, financiers, music supervisors, composers and casting directors.

The events are then broadcast on the Internet at LA Live, a premiere webcaster of live film and music events in Los Angeles. The online site is designed for industry representatives who cannot attend screenings.

Hollywood Shorts hasn't been around that long, but their energy and ability to make things happen bodes well. If you are in Los Angeles, you might want to check them out. They said they champion directors, writers and actors.

Hollywood Shorts/Kimberley Browning
11166 Burbank Blvd.
North Hollywood, CA 91601
310-358-7634
Website: www.lalive.com/hollywoodshorts
E-mail: grifplace@aol.com

Actors in Playwrighting Groups

The life blood of the theater is new material, so several theaters in the New York and Los Angeles theatrical community offer developmental possibilities for new playwrights.

Writers are the very people you want to support and get to know since they are writing the material you will want to work on. A good way to do this is to call these groups, ask if they use actors to read material at their meetings and volunteer your services.

Playwrights Horizons/New York — One of Manhattan's most prestigious Off-Broadway theaters presents new playwrights on a regular basis.

Playwrights Horizons/Sonya Sobieski
416 W 42nd St.
New York, NY 10036
212-564-1235

Ensemble Studio Theater — EST produces many
new plays, sponsors new play festivals as well as week
and weekend summer workshops in the Catskills in
addition to their ongoing playwrighting groups.

Ensemble Studio Theater/Eileen Meyers
Literary Department
549 W 52nd St.
New York, NY 10019
212-581-9603

The Public Theater — New York's most famous
off-Broadway theater has helped develop such plays as
Sticks and Bones, A Chorus Line and *Hair.* Connected and
fearless, The Public also has ongoing playwright groups.

The Public Theater/First Stages
425 Lafayette Ave.
New York, NY 10003
212-539-8500
Website: http://www.publictheater.org/index2.htm

New Dramatists — New Dramatists offers a host
of support for scriptwriters: screenplay development,
musical theater workshops; writers' workspaces and a
summer playwriting residency in Lake Placid, NY. With
all that material being developed, they must need some
actors.

New Dramatists
424 W 44th St.
New York, NY 10036
212-757-6960
Website: http://www.itp.tsoa.nyu.edu/~diana/ndintro.html
E-mail: Newdram@aol.com

The Audrey Skirball Theater — Los Angeles ASK theater not only spends its time and money developing and encouraging playwrights, they support and encourage actors by paying them for readings. They also have a website listing all Los Angeles playwrighting groups: http://www.askplay.org/guides/pgdindex.html

ASK Theater Projects
11845 W Olympic Blvd.
Los Angeles, CA 90064
310-478-3200
Website: http://www.askplays.org
E-mail: askplay@primenet.com

Playwrights Kitchen Ensemble — Housed at the Coronet Theater near the Beverly Center in Los Angeles, PKE was founded by Dan Lauria (who played the dad on *The Wonder Years*) and sponsors a Monday Night Play Reading series featuring star actors reading new scripts.

Since the inauguration of the series in 1990, The Playwrights Kitchen Ensemble has read over 300 new plays. PKE annually considers over 1,000 plays for the 48 or so readings held during the year.

In addition to the play reading series, there are two fee based writing workshops that meet once a week. Actors read 10-25 pages of a work-in-progress so that writers can hear their work aloud. The cost is $300 per year for playwrights and $5 monthly for actors.

Each workshop is limited to 18 writers and 18 actors. The Monday Night Play Reading series only presents material written specifically for the stage, but the workshops feature material for stage, film and television.

Material for the stage developed at the workshops is considered for the Monday night readings. Director Ted Weiant, actor-director Richard Zavaglia and playwright Joe Cacaci all administer the program. Ted Rawlins, who founded the American Stage Company in Teaneck, New Jersey, has come on board as the executive director at PKE. John Bunzel is the contact person for the playwrighting group.

PKE/Playwrights Kitchen Ensemble
John Bunzel/Coronet Theater
368 N La Cienega Ave.
Los Angeles, CA 90048
818-980-3641

Other Resources

The International Theater Institute is an organization
started in 1948 by UNESCO committed to foster theater
communication with 82 centers around the world. Not
only a conduit for information, ITI provides entree for
artists of all kinds (actors, writers, directors, etc.) who are
either going abroad or considering it.

Sometime in 1999, ITI will fold its business into
the larger and better funded Theater Communications
Group. All of ITI's assets will be available via CTG. As
of this writing, there is no decision as to the name of the
merged group. I will list both addresses. The number
listed is current, but may change after the move.

ITI puts out a quarterly newsletter that's yours
for a contribution and maintains an extensive research
library which is available to anyone doing serious
research:

The International Theater Institute @ TCG
Louis A. Rachow (pronounced Rock-Oh)
355 Lexington Ave. (at 40th St.)
New York, NY 10017
212-697-5230

Louis turned me onto some great reference books:

The Original British Theater Directory
Richmond House Publishing Co. Ltd.
9-11 Richmond Buildings, London IV5AF
44-071-437-9556/fax 44-071-434-0200

The British Alternative Theater Directory
Rebecca Books
Ivor House, Suite #2
1 Bridge St.
Cardiff CF12TH Wales
44-022-237-8452

The Performing Arts Yearbook for Europe
Arts Publishing International, Ltd.
4 Assam St.
London E17QS
44-071-247-0066/fax 44-071-247-6868

Price listed on the cover is in pounds sterling
with no U.S. equivalent, but Louis says *The Performing Arts
Yearbook for Europe* is roughly $50 and the other books
listed are about $30 each. As you can see, they are
expensive, but can be read at the ITI library.

American Theater Works

American Theater Works is a non-profit
corporation for the performing arts located in Dorset,
Vermont. ATW encompasses three distinct programs: an
audition and hiring center for actors, production and
management staff, their Equity theater and a program for
apprentices and interns.

They also produce two excellent resource books:
The Summer Theater Directory and *The Regional Theater
Directory* written by Jill Charles. You can buy directly from
Jill or at your local theatrical bookshop.

Jill Charles
PO Box 510
Dorset, VT 05251-0510
802-867-2223
Website: www.Theatredirectories.com
E-mail: theater @sover.net

Repertory Theater Websites

An Internet search using Infoseek and typing in the search menu: (repertory theater) brought up more addresses than I can print here. I'm listing a few for you, but if you are looking for a job, I'd check out all these websites and see what all is going on. Some of these sites list internship possibilities.

Actor's Theater of Louiseville, KY
http://www.actorstheater.org/

The Alley Theater, Houston, TX
http://www.alleytheater.com/

American Conservatory Theater, San Francisco, CA
http://www.act-sfbay.org/about/index.html

Denver Performing Arts Complex, Denver, CO
http://denver.sidewalk.com/link/10881

Providence Black Repertory Company, Providence, RI
http://www.oso.com/community/groups/prblkrep

Seattle Repertory Theater, Seattle, WA
http://www.seattlerep.org/

South Coast Repertory, Costa Mesa, CA
http://www.scr.org/

Spanish Theater Repertory (Repertorio Español), NY, NY
http://www.geocities.com/Broadway/8369/nfindex.html

The Studio Upstairs Theater Repertory, Goshen, NY.
http://www.studioupstairs.com/

Threshold Theater Newtonville, MA
http://www.theatermirror.com/threshold/

Hollywood Casting Search Center

Another online resource is Hollywood Casting Search Center. HCSC bill themselves as the world's premier Internet-based talent system. Casting jobs are listed and job wanted ads posted. This looks to me to be most helpful if you are looking for non-union work. I checked out the current listings. A couple looked promising, but mostly it was composed of the resumes of a few serious actors and a smattering of goof-balls who listed their resumes about 100 times.

It's free though, you might want to check it out: http://www.hollywoodweb.com.

As always, don't be starry-eyed. Look with a degree of skepticism at promises of fame and fortune no matter where they come from. We all want to believe fairytales, but there is really no easy way to accomplish anything other than one step at a time.

Search Engines to Find Local Agents

Power up a search engine and type in *talent agents + your city* and see what you find. I was also able to access casting director numbers as well as agents and actors in places as diverse as London and Des Moines. The possibilities are endless.

You can look up film companies the same way. I typed in *film production companies + Iowa* and came up with:

◆   *dhg Productions, Inc., located in Des Moines, Iowa,*

works with companies across the country to provide corporate video and commercial spot production. We also handle multimedia projects as diverse as touch-screen menus for kiosks and trade show displays.

If I lived in the Des Moines area and was looking for work, I'd make a phone call to dhg and ask if they hired actors for their films.

There's Always the Yellow Pages

Whether you are in Podunk, New York or Los Angeles, you have to make your own opportunities.

People think job seeking as an actor is not exactly like looking in the help wanted section of your newspaper or looking in the Yellow Pages but it is.

I went to the library and looked in the Yellow Pages at a cross section of phone books to check showbiz employment possibilities. I looked up St. Paul, MN; Des Moines, IA; Phoenix, AZ and Tacoma, WA.

The Yellow Pages of each of these cities listed Entertainers and Entertainment Agencies. The biggest possibilities involved singers, (there were lots of musical and variety agents) comedians, magicians, etc.

Some listed speakers and most listed those services having to do with conventions and fairs. Phoenix listed something called *Ladies Choice* (your guess is as good as mine). *The Bag Lady* in Tacoma also piqued my curiosity.

Get in the habit of scanning the classified and entertainment sections of your newspaper. That's where you will see casting notices for local production companies as well as major motion pictures that might be locationing in your area.

Be Bold

In the meantime, go for it. When you see in your newspaper that a theater group is casting, go there. Try out for something. Find out the name of the play; buy a copy and read it. If you are right for a part, select the scene that shows that character best and learn it. Get a friend to read it with you and be prepared to read that scene when you arrive.

If management wants you to do a different scene, don't be afraid to suggest the one you are familiar with. They will probably let you do it. If not, ask for 20 minutes to work on the alternate scene before reading. *Do not* read cold. You will never do as well as if you had prepared the material. No matter how well you think you are able to cold read, it will never be the work you could do if you were able to prepare ahead of time.

If you sing, offer your services at church or at a Lions Club Dinner. Wherever something is happening, become a part of it. Be the master of ceremonies at the charity auction or be the host who greets everybody. Take every opportunity to get up in front of people, no matter how menial and you'll find that with experience comes heightened self esteem as well as skill. People will begin to think of you as the person who helps make their event work. If nothing is happening, find a way to stimulate some activity. If you get tired of being the one who always starts the merry-go-round, you are in the wrong business.

Perspective

It's difficult to know, when you are working on a project, whether it and you are very good. You have to believe in your work in order to invest your energies 100%, so sometimes we develop a little myopia along the way. That's why it's always good to invite at least one friend whose judgement and taste you trust, to see your work before you invite an agent, manager or casting director. You're only new once. Since people tend to remember first encounters, do your best to make sure yours is a good one.

Hopefully, you've made a decision by now to

take things as they come: acting, directing, producing, casting, etc., and in following these roads, you'll find fulfillment in show business.

You've organized your life, your home, your business space and your way of thinking. You have a specific plan about how you are going to go about creating work for yourself. You now know how to research your marketplace for showbiz jobs of every stripe. You know about agents and unions. You have a support group.

Use that feedback. Knowing your strengths as well as your weaknesses gives you power. Monitor your progress regularly. Make a check list with a point numerical point system. Over time, you'll be able to see your progress in various areas. Reviewing the check list when you're feeling down will enable you to see how far you have come.

Getting and Taking a Meeting

It's preferable to send a note to a potential employer that precedes a picture and resume. Pictures and resumes may sit in a pile by the door waiting until it's *look at the pictures and resumes* day. Letters are opened immediately. Particularly those that are on good paper and are typed.

Last year I met a lovely young actress. I saw her work a time or two and thought she showed some promise. One day she showed me the letter she was sending out to casting directors. I knew immediately one of the reasons she was not getting their attention.

The paper looked like the cheapest dime store note paper and her handwriting looked like it belonged to someone in primary school. While it is not a sin to have sub-standard handwriting and cheap paper, it does not demand you be taken seriously. Do without something else and invest in good paper and a typewriter or go to a copy center and pay to have the letter typed.

When you actually do get someone's attention and

have a meeting (as opposed to an audition) there are several things to attend to in addition to spiffing up your resume and praying.

Make sure your shoes are polished. Your clothes don't have to be expensive, but they should be clean, well pressed and in good repair. The care you take with your person projects the care you take in general and will be the key to how you are perceived.

♦   *When men dress casually — they lose some of their authority; when women do the same, they lose most of theirs.*

Even within the confines of casual dress, the folks in charge figure out how to display their rank and power. Maybe it's linen slacks and $800 Italian loafers on dress-down Friday, or a crisp jacket over that snazzy sleeveless dress. Walk into any company on casual day and chances are you'll have no trouble figuring out who runs the show.

No matter what the dress code says, the old rule of thumb still applies; Don't dress for the job you have today, dress for the one you want tomorrow.

Naked Ambition
Marla Dickerson
The Los Angeles Times
August 10, 1998

Make sure your handshake is strong and that you have something interesting to talk about. If there's a bowling trophy on a table, mention that your father bowled. Don't lie, but find an authentic way to connect.

Sit back in the chair, don't slump. They may be buying an actor who is going to play a bum, but they want to know that the actor is strong, has his own ideas and is unafraid.

Employers are putting a property in an actor's hands. It is a huge responsibility and demands a great deal of energy. If you are playing the leading role and you are frightened and don't have a vision of how to do it, they do not want to know that. This is as true for an executive at IBM as it is for an actor.

After the meeting and/or audition, sit down and make a list of all the things you did well and all the things you could have done better. Review this material before the next meeting. It will pay off.

Get Used to It

The bad news is that this constant selling is never over. You may as well face the facts now as later. Your whole career is going to be spent making people think they must employ you. Yes, there will be those times when you are semi-regularly employed, but the bottom line is that you are a self-employed person. You are responsible for keeping the momentum going once you get it started.

Careers go through moments of heat when they appear to sustain themselves, but don't lose your fire starting skills; for as night follows day, cold follows heat and you'll be in the momentum starting business again.

Going In

Once you have done all your homework and feel ready to begin, it's time to set goals and begin being businesslike about creating your own work. You're ready to call on advertising agencies, television stations, film companies, promotional organizations, casting directors, directors and/or producers.

Remember, in this business, packaging is just as important as content.

Wrap Up

✓   take care of business
✓   respond to good work
✓   have patience
✓   enjoy the process
✓   deal with rejection constructively
✓   keep perspective
✓   generate publicity

- ✓ cultivate relationships with the casting community
- ✓ cultivate relationships with fans
- ✓ get pictures and resumes
- ✓ check for phone messages often
- ✓ learn how to look for work
- ✓ realistically evaluate your work before inviting scrutiny
- ✓ be open to whatever comes your way
- ✓ utilize your support groups
- ✓ monitor your progress realistically
- ✓ packaging is just as important as content

11   Auditioning & the Way It Really Is

After all your hard work, you have progressed beyond trying to get someone's attention, to having a meeting with them, to actually being called to audition.

All auditions are different. Sometimes there will be only a casting director who will read with you, but sometimes the producers and directors are there with the casting director. In Los Angeles, there might be 20 people in the room when you audition. At first glance, seeing all those people might rattle you, but if you take the attitude of *Oh boy! It's a bigger audience!* you'll be using the circumstances to your advantage.

In most markets, the casting director holds preliminary auditions, selects those considered most appropriate and calls these people back to be reviewed by the director and/or producer. Sometimes the preliminary audition is taped and those tapes are shown to the buyers who make decisions regarding callbacks.

Auditions can take many forms. Commercial auditions traditionally entail many, many actors who are called to read for a casting director and/or producers and/or directors, usually in a conference room.

Theatrical auditions are frequently held onstage in a theater, but are also regularly held in meeting rooms when a theater is unavailable. It might be important for you to find out before the audition just where it will be held. Your preparation might be different for a small office than for a large theater.

Film and television auditions are usually held in a meeting room. If your work is not already known by the casting director, she will screen you before presenting you to the producers and/or directors.

Two inspiring books about auditioning that you may find helpful are *Audition* by Michael Shurtleff and *Next* by casting directors, Ellie Kanner and Paul G. Bens.

Shurtleff's book was so supportive and instructive that I wanted to sleep with it under my pillow.

His descriptions of Barbra Streisand's early auditions alone are worth the price of the book.

The Kanner/Bens book not only covers audition behavior, but answers questions about deal memos and being replaced.

Preparation

Prepare carefully. If you don't want the job, don't go. You won't do your best work and there is no way of erasing a bad impression from a room full of people who just saw you do bad work. You never know who is sitting in and when they might have a job that you would be right for. People remember.

A few months ago I got a job for which I didn't audition. I scanned the list of people involved with the project, searching for a familiar name. How had I gotten this job? On the set, the director reminded me that we had worked together seven years ago. I had one scene on a TV movie that I couldn't remember. He did.

Each actor has his own way of attacking a project. Even if you are going to read only a few lines, it is worth every effort to get your hands on the material ahead of time and read the entire script at least twice before focusing on your scene.

It means everything to me to be able to read the material aloud with another human being prior to the audition. Sometimes there is no one around to do this with and I just have to take my best shot. I have been known to pay the neighborhood kids to read lines with me. I just pay their babysitting rate. Some people work with other actors and take that actor along with them to the audition.

If you are to provide your own material, choose carefully. Unless specifically asked, do not bring Shakespeare or another classic. These parts will not show your castability. No matter how well you do it, the material makes the primary impression so if you can entertain and charm them with an appealing script, your chances are better. Actors win Academy Awards every year for being lucky enough to get the role that shows them to their best advantage.

When I was a student of Herbert Berghof's at the HB Studios in New York, he used to suggest that the best material for an actor was from novels and plays written by an author from the actor's own region and background. It's not that difficult to choose scenes from a novel and write phrases that bridge the dialogue if it does not stand as is. When you work with material written by an author raised with your same sensibilities, you will bring an unconscious truth that cannot be acted and when you work from a novel, you have material that is more interesting to your auditioners because of it's originality.

It's not wise to do memorable scenes associated with famous actors. You may be really fabulous, but while you are doing Robert DeNiro's role in *Taxi Driver*, the producers are wishing Mr. DeNiro was present.

When you prepare for the audition, make sure you are specific. Whatever is in your mind when you are doing the scene will show. If confusion and fear are your primary concerns instead of the emotion of the scene and the lines are only coming out of your mouth without access to your brain, confusion and fear will be the message they receive.

Although there is a difference of opinion about dressing for the part for an audition, I always do (within reason). I don't do it for them; I do it for me. Dressing in character helps feed my feelings for the scene. As you dress, think about how your character would go about dressing and how the character feels.

Another facet of auditioning (and acting, of course) is character. If you come in with a character over and above what is written, whether it is an attitude, a walk or a way of speaking, you will stand out head and shoulders from the crowd.

The reason that so many stand-up comedians get work is that most have honed a character that they play in their act. Writers come in, see the act, steal the most interesting characteristics and write them into their scripts and sometimes, the comedian becomes part of the project.

Peter Boyle had been working for many years when he captured the attention of the world in a film called *Joe*. The words and basic value system of that character were written into the script, but in fact, Peter had invented a blue collar character that he had been playing for years in various skits at *Second City* (a famous improvisational group in Chicago). When he got the chance to play *Joe*, he plugged in the character material he had been working on for years.

If you haven't worked on creating characters, start now and add dimension to your work.

Auditioning and Waiting

In college, you only have to wait ten minutes for a full professor before you can walk. I don't give much more time to casting directors and producers unless there are extenuating circumstances. If the casting director explains the problem and apologizes, I am able to be good natured about it up to a point. After 15 minutes with no word from on high, I find a telephone, call my agent and have him deal with it. He may tell me to leave or he may make a phone call that results in the casting director apologizing, getting me right in or making another appointment.

If you are a member of Screen Actors Guild, the client must pay an hourly rate if he keeps you waiting past one hour. Don't make a fuss, just jot down the names of some of the other waiting actors from the sign-in sheet, call SAG, mention the incident plus the other names (so the client won't be able to single out that you are the one who called) and you will ultimately get a check in the mail. It will be for one hour pro-rated from SAG minimum for an eight-hour day.

Even if you are going to get paid, it's still hard to stay in a good humor, so don't wait so long that you get huffy. If you get testy, you are dead in the water, so go ahead and leave. They're not going to want to hire an angry actor. If you are Tom Cruise or Julia Roberts, you can get by with throwing a tantrum, otherwise, forget about it. Explain that you have another audition and that you will be happy to come back. Be sure to address this before you get irritable and when you will still be happy to come back.

The longer you wait, the more your energy is dissipated by holding the anger down. It is a real test of my mettle to put aside the anger at being kept waiting and still do a good audition.

Dr. Spock says that if a child has a tantrum, it is the parent's fault. The parent's job is to notice the signs that precede a tantrum and take steps to head it off. I try to be as caring a parent to myself as I was to my children. Therefore, I walk out of bad situations.

Audition Behavior

You are judged from the moment you enter the audition office. Receptionists are sometimes quite powerful so be sure to acknowledge them. You don't have to be phony, but this is a human being here who doesn't appreciate being invisible any more than you do.

When you enter the audition room, take a moment to adjust to the atmosphere. Don't waste time, but take a few seconds to breathe. Notice who is there and what is going on. Make sure you have something interesting to say if you're called upon to chat.

You can talk about the World Series, the Super Bowl, the Oscars or the weather. Don't be inane, but take a moment. You will feel more comfortable and so will they. This is also part of the audition. They have scheduled this time for you because they think you are worth looking at. Take the time.

Don't be afraid to move around. Set up the room as you want. Go over the scene in your mind as you physically take in the room to visualize yourself in the scene. The casting director will be happy to take the cue from you about when to begin the scene. If she begins the scene before you are ready, just say you need another moment to prepare. Turn your back, get in character, remember what went on in the script in the moment just before this scene and begin with that energy.

Insecurity

Some actors think they take the edge off their insecurity and humanize themselves by commenting on their fears in the audition room. Insecurity is not appealing to the buyer. There is too much money at stake. No one wants to hear about your impending nervous breakdown. They're worried about their own and they want to feel that they have found the actor that is going to solve all their problems, not present new ones.

In her autobiography, Elizabeth Ashley speaks of a time in her career when she was really hot. She was hired for a film and suggested her acting teacher, Sydney Pollack, who had never directed. Before shooting began, she saw a screening of *Ship of Fools* and decided that her work was bad. She invited Pollack to lunch and told him her work in *Fools* was bad and that she would need all his help in order to do a good job in their approaching film. Pollack conveyed the information to his agents who also represented Anne Bancroft. Phone calls were exchanged and somehow Ashley was out and Bancroft was in. Ashley says she never recovered:

✦   *It broke me. And the thing that broke me was not the hustlers and the handlers, and it wasn't the hard, mean way of doing business. It was that I had thought there was some ground where it was safe to tell the truth, to be afraid and say, "I don't know," and there wasn't. I doubted myself and was looking for help and you don't get to do that. There's no place for that. If you don't know, tell the bastards you do.*
        Actress: *Postcards from the Road*
        Elizabeth Ashley
        M. Evans & Company
        New York

Some actors speak of being so frightened at an audition that they didn't do their best. It's all very well and good for others to say, *just relax*, but it's not that easy. That's one of the reasons it is so important to get up and perform at every opportunity. The more time you spend in front of people, the less you will be frightened.

The best way to give up your anxiety is to be so specific and concentrated in your work that you don't have time for anxiety to creep in. It takes enormous effort to really focus and take yourself out of the audition room and into the material. You can only do this by constantly exercising your muscles of concentration.

Every day take time to visualize something. Either the material you are working on or something that you want. Use your mind to emotionally visit the situation. If you are picturing a job, then see yourself already having it. Feel what you would feel under those circumstances. Then in a pressured audition situation, those tools are ready for you to use.

Working with props is a good example of how effective concentration can take anxiety away. Props require authentic attention to use appropriately; threading a needle, peeling a potato, washing a dish, or repairing a stool have to be done in reality or the task won't work. That reality grounds the actor into the scene.

Memorizing the Material

There are several schools of thought about memorizing the material for an audition. My own personal preference, which many casting directors say is a bad idea, is to commit the scene to memory. It's not that difficult for me to do and I feel I do a much better job if I can free myself from the page. There have been times that it didn't work out, but I'm still not sorry I go for it. Frequently, I will announce that I am going to attempt a scene without the script and that if it doesn't work out I will use it. And sometimes I have had to.

If you do not have an easy time memorizing,

don't go for it. A few years ago, I was conducting a seminar for The American Film Institute on *Auditioning and the Business of Show Business* and I gave audition material out on Saturday night for simulated auditions on Sunday. One of the actresses had put down her script for her *audition*. She failed to impress me in any way. In a later part of the session, I gave her some material that she had only a few minutes to prepare so there was no possibility of her memorizing it. She was a completely different actress when her energy was freed from the obligation to memorize. Do what works best for you.

Casting directors tell me it's not only all right, but a very good idea to stop an audition that is going badly and begin again. Apologies are bad form, just smile and do better.

Negotiating

Although getting chosen is a big step towards a job, it doesn't necessarily mean you are going to work. The next hurtle is negotiation. Money, billing and working rules are laid down.

If you are in one of the performing unions, many details are already addressed in a standard contact. Whatever is not already spelled out must be negotiated. As a beginning actor, one usually is happy to do anything for any pittance, frequently for free. The actor should look upon the free work as graduate school.

When you are farther along in your profession, you will find that there are three plums possible in any job: billing, money and part. You will want to get at least one of them.

If the part stinks and the money is terrible but your billing is going to be better than you have gotten in the past, that might be a reason to take the job. If you are to get little money, and no billing, but the part is sensational, for heaven's sake take the job! Maybe all that appeals to you is the money. That's not all bad, either.

Let's talk a little bit about money. Until July 1999,

scale for a day working through Screen Actors Guild is $576. A three-day contract pays $1,900 and weekly (film or television) is $2,700. Half-hour television episodes are usually shot in five days.

Past minimum is a category called major role performer which involves any actor who negotiates credit before the show or on a separate card or its equivalent in a crawl at the end of the show. There is a provision in the current Television Agreement requiring a certain level of minimum payment for major role performers (also called guest stars or Top of the Show).

The minimums guarantee five days of pay for a half hour show at not less than $2,880, as of 7/1/1998; $2,980 as of 7/1/1999, $3,035 as of 7/1/2000 and eight days of pay for a one-hour show at not less than $4,608 as of 7/1/1998; $4,768 as of 7/1/1999, $4,856 as of 7/1/2000.

Until the major role performer category, most actors never noticed that what used to be referred to as Top of the Show (the so-called top that any show would negotiate for guest stars other than big names) was only a few dollars more than minimum for a week. Actors happily accepted top of the show thinking this somehow put them into an elite classification. The day that real working actors got on the Screen Actors Guild Board of Directors, they brought the major performer category into the next negotiation with producers. It's not a large gain, but it is something.

A casting director recently told me that although her show strongly resisted paying more than top of show to anyone, she was able to get away with paying just a few dollars more because most actors didn't know the rates and just needed to hear that they were getting paid more than Top of the Show. Do yourself a favor and be alert to fees and arithmetic.

Clearly, there are performers who make much more than top even though the producers swear it isn't so. It is their way of price-fixing. In any event, salaries are always what the traffic will bear once you graduate past minimum. If you are hot or you don't want the job, you can demand more. Nothing makes an actor more attractive to a casting director than not wanting the job. The longer you say no, the higher the fee becomes.

There is a point beyond which the casting director will not go. If you want to get your price up, judgment is everything. As in poker, you want your adversary to put as much money on the table as possible, but you don't want him to fold.

When you really need the job, it's more difficult to take the chance involved in tough negotiations.

Series regulars (with no important credits) usually work their first half-hour series for $5,000 per show. Series regulars who are visible command much more money. One of the reasons *Dallas* finally went off the air was that Larry Hagman and the other regulars had (after 11 years) negotiated their salaries to such astronomical heights that the show was just too expensive to produce.

Quotes/Money

Quotes refer to the amount of money you were paid for your last job. If you have been paid $5,000 per week on a movie of the week or $1,500 per day on a film, these fees are your *quotes*. You use your quotes in negotiation citing where, when and for whom you made this money in order to get paid at least that much again. Be truthful because casting directors will check. Part of their job is to get the best talent for the least amount of money.

All the casting directors know one another and share information. Actors should share, also. It would be important to you to know that John Somebody made $2,000 for a day on a particular show. When you ask for $1,500 and they say, *we never pay that much*, you'd know they're not playing square with you. Never divulge your sources of information, however, or you will lose them.

If you have been working on a per day basis at minimum, doing good work and getting good feedback for a period of time, it might be time to start asking for

$750 a day and then more. If you are unsuccessful in moving your price up, just amass some more good credits and try again. It will happen.

A friend of mine determined that he would no longer work for major role/top of the show money. Although not a star, my friend works a lot, has a very special quality and felt he deserved more. In fact, he has been able to demand double top a couple of times, but the number of times per year that he has worked has dropped dramatically. You may have to decide whether you want to work more often or get paid more.

The following quote is from 1992, but the information is still timely.

✦ *Casting directors are telling agents, "Get me the best actors for the least money. Don't submit anyone who won't work for scale plus ten percent." As a result, mid-priced actors have seen salaries drop as much as 50 percent, with no room for negotiation. Top of the show pay for TV guest performers is lower now than it was 10 years ago, and more name actors are competing for ever fewer guest spots. Series regulars have taken pay freezes and even cuts in order to keep their jobs. Disney just announced that the studio will not pay more than $25,000 per episode to series stars.*
Bad News
Compiled by Mark Locher
Screen Actor
Spring, 1992, Volume 31, No. 1

You might be offered the part of your dreams, but the money is terrible. Though you have painstakingly increased your quote, you are now offered the perfect part for very little money. By all means, take the part and ask the casting director to offer you a *no quote*. This is exactly what it says. If another casting director tries to obtain information regarding your pay on that job, the information is unavailable. It seems to me, however, that if you have a *no quote* the casting director must assume that you worked for less than your usual fee.

Getting Hired

This is not a business of absolutes. As I've said before, there is luck involved. Part of playing this particular poker game is training yourself as consistently and thoroughly as possible. Study acting, singing, dancing, dialects, and fencing. The more things you are trained to do, the more parts you can be considered for.

Training and ability are a given once you are recognized as part of the talent pool. You and your competitors are all good at your work and the decision will be made on a variety of things.

Getting Replaced

Getting the job and beginning rehearsal is no guarantee you will actually work the job, although, if it is a union job, you will be paid.

When I was starring on a series called *Joe's World* for NBC, I began to realize how lucky I had been in my career. We would frequently meet for the first day of rehearsal, read around the table with the guest cast and by the time we got back from lunch, we might be missing two guest cast members. Management somehow didn't think they were funny enough at the first reading. The moral here is to always put your best foot forward. There is too much money at stake and people are too paranoid for faith. You must always be showing people what you can do.

It's also not uncommon to land a pilot, work the show and be replaced when the show comes to series. Sometimes it is because the actor they originally wanted has become available. Sometimes their fantasies did not turn out to be the same as your reality. It's childish to take it as a sign that you are untalented and will surely never work again. Just examine the situation and see if there is something you might have done differently with either the people or the material. Learn and get on with it; it's self indulgent and mean to beat yourself up.

Factors Involved in Staying Hired

People commonly think of professional behavior as being on time, learning your lines, not eating garlic and using deodorant. There are other essential things that no one ever thinks to tell you.

Don't keep people waiting. If you are on a set, and the director or stage manager calls for you, don't finish the joke or story you are telling. Explain to whoever that you will finish later. It is a temptation to entertain on the set, particularly if you know the latest gossip, funniest joke, etc., but three minutes here and five minutes there do add up. If you are on a film or television set, you could be holding up an enormous group of people. Not only is it expensive, it is arrogant to consider that your joke (which only five people are going to hear, anyway) is important enough to keep 150 people waiting.

Don't clown around. Before entering college, I had no prior experience as an actress except for school plays at a very minor level. When I got to college, it seemed like heaven. I really wanted to be liked and chose to become a real clown at rehearsals. One day, as I was delaying rehearsals doing some funny thing, not saying the line properly to get a laugh, or whatever, I looked across the stage to my friend, Jerry Melton. Jerry was older and a much more experienced actor than I and I really looked up to him. As I looked at him, he made this face that said: *No, no. Don't do that. It's not cool.*

I got it immediately and stopped. No one had ever told me and I was young and dumb. I found out later that I had not been cast in a couple of plays because I was known as someone who wasted time.

Stay off the telephone. Stay tuned in. I guested on a television show that had a lot of young actors as leads. They varied in ages from 6 to 21. The show was not doing well for a variety of reasons, but it was also woefully behind schedule because every time the cameras were ready to roll, one or another of the young stars was on the phone. It took time to get them off the phone and back to the set.

Others who might have been more conscientious and stayed close to the set saw no future in that since the set-ups were always delayed, so they started straggling about and had to be rounded up as well. Yes, it is up to the Assistant Directors and Stage Managers to make sure the actors are in their places when the camera is ready to roll, but it isn't their job to give actors lessons in manners. It's unlikely that anyone is ever going to take the time to explain to you that you are wasting everyone's time, that your energies are focused on phone calls instead of the work at hand and that because of these things, the producers just won't be motivated to request you on future projects.

I was able to see myself in these actors and thought of the times that I had rushed to the phone between shots instead of staying tuned to the set and wondered not only how many people I might have alienated by this behavior, but how my work might have been affected as well.

I have a friend who is on a Top 10 television show. She has very little to do each week. She spends lots of time in her dressing room while the rest of the cast is rehearsing without her. She might have three hours off in the afternoon.

But she never rushes out to shop or takes long lunches. She doesn't spend all the time in her dressing room on her script, but she tells me that if she were to leave the studio, she would not be focused on her work. She needs to be there.

I think of another actress I know on a highly-regarded show. She doesn't have much to do, either. The difference is this: she is so angry because she feels under-utilized that she doesn't ever prepare well. Sometimes, not at all. It's only a few lines. Who needs to work on it? The result is the writers perceive this and have no incentive to write for her. She doesn't do what she is given very well, so why give her more?

Wherever you are, if you are not part of the

solution, you are part of the problem.

Whatever capacity you are working in, the employer wants to know you care and that you want the whole endeavor to be the best possible product. I am never happy to pay someone to do the minimum, but it's a pleasure to pay someone money I feel they have earned and it's to my advantage to reward them with more work.

Being Right for the Part/Visibility

When a casting director speaks of an actor as right for a part, he is speaking about the essence of the actor. We all associate a particular essence with Tom Cruise and a different essence with Jim Carrey, so one would not expect Jim Carrey and Tom Cruise to be up for the same part.

Another aspect of being right concerns visibility. Visibility means currently being on view in film, theater or television. In this business, it is out of sight, out of mind. You can be a dead ringer for Brad Pitt, but if you are not as visible as he is, you're not going to get seen for his part. The bigger the part, the bigger the credits you must to have to support being seen.

The third element of right has to do with physicality. If you are 6'7" and everyone else in the project is 5'4", it does seem unlikely you will be hired. If they are putting together a family, it is necessary that you look more like the rest of the family than your closest competitor, all other things being equal.

Protocol

Afraid of doing the wrong thing, when I first worked on a set in Los Angeles, I would quietly go to my chair and sit until someone decided to speak to me. As it turned out, I now realize, this is the most appropriate way to behave.

On a film or television set, there is an unspoken hierarchy or pecking order. By and large, an extra does not go up to a star or director and begin a conversation. Neither does a supporting player, unless there is already a relationship. The star and director can approach anyone they choose. Others best wait to be recognized. It's very subtle, but very real.

There's nothing wrong with this. It's etiquette in the business. Just be cool and observe. You will understand quickly. I don't imagine a lowly secretary goes up to the President of IBM and starts a discussion either. When you become the star, it will be up to you to make others feel at home on the set.

Reporting to Work

For those of you who have never had the opportunity to work on a film or television set, let me give you a idea of what it is like. If you guest on a television series, you will encounter a family of actors who have been working together and who have already bonded. In most cases, they will be welcoming and warm and treat you well. You will, however, be a guest and as in any other family, not an intimate member of the group. It is wise to remember this and wait to be invited to partake in whatever their normal rituals might be.

When you arrive, the AD will show you to your dressing room, advise you when hair and make-up will be ready for you and possibly ask what you might like for breakfast if it is really early in the morning.

Hair and make-up will have an idea of how you should look since they have read the script, but remember, you know how you look best. It's best to address things up front; *How do you see this character? I normally wear my hair this way. I usually do minimal make-up, I like my eyes done this way, etc.* Be tactful in making suggestions. Although hair and make-up want you to be comfortable, they don't like to be bossed around.

You will have already met with wardrobe for fittings or have been advised regarding which of your own clothing might be appropriate. You'll get dressed and either stay in your dressing room relaxing or report to the set. It's perfectly all right to wait to be called to the set. I usually go on to the set as soon as I am ready because I want to bond with everybody and become comfortable on the set as soon as possible.

The prop man will usually show you a chair marked *Cast* for you to sit in and you'll hang out until they call you to rehearse or shoot. After a shot or rehearsal when you have twenty minutes or more before the next shot, many people run to the telephone. If you need to make a call, do so, but keep it short. There is usually one phone for at least a hundred people, so be considerate and don't make unnecessary calls. You should be focused on your work, anyway.

There is always a table filled with munchie food of one kind or another. Eat as much as you like, but remember the energy it takes to digest that food is energy you can use to focus on your work and harness your emotional life. The more you can stay focused on the work, the better off you will be. It's good to fraternize with your fellow actors, but remember to focus on your work. It may feel good to be adorable and tell your best story, but when the AD calls you to shoot, it can be difficult to quickly adjust to what's happening in the scene.

Between set-ups and after lunch, hair and make-up will check you. Make sure you are always where someone can find you. If you must leave the set to go to the bathroom or change, speak to one of the ADs to make sure there is time before you are needed again and to let them know where you will be. If you are in the middle of a shot and need to go to the bathroom, try to wait until that shot is complete, otherwise, there may be 100 people standing around waiting for you to return. It may not look that way, and the AD will say *Go ahead and go*, but the result is, the shot is delayed.

When you have finished your work for the day, the AD will release you and you will be given a sign out sheet. When you go to your dressing room to change, you'll leave your wardrobe in your dressing room. The wardrobe people are not paid to be maids and/or butlers, so be sure to hang your clothes up before you leave.

Situation Comedies

A situation comedy is completely different. On the first day, the entire cast and staff sit around a large table while the cast reads the script. There is usually a table with breakfast type foods available and people are casual. The regular cast can afford that behavior, you can't. So be alert, pleasant and do your best work.

After the read through, there will be a break while the director and writers confer about what worked and what didn't. At that point, the writers and producers depart to begin rewrites and the director usually begins blocking. Most shows will do a run through for the writers and producers at the end of the day. That night the changes will be messengered to your home so that you will be prepared for the next day's work.

On the fourth day of a taped show, you will spend the day walking the material slowly so that the camera people can mark their moves. At the end of that day, there will be a dress rehearsal with full wardrobe and on camera so the producers can see what is happening. On filmed shows, they will usually begin filming part of the show on that day.

On the fifth day, you will get a later call (since you will be there into evening if there is an audience), report to hair and make-up, put on your wardrobe and go out in front of an audience and do the show. There will be a break for dinner. There might be line changes and then everyone prepares for the second show. After the second show, the audience will leave and any *pickups* (scenes that need repair) will be re-shot. You might get out by 10 PM if the show is organized and has been shooting for several seasons or it could be midnight.

For feature and television films, the drill is much like my description of life on a television series set. If you are lucky enough to have a good part, necessitating several days or weeks of work, you will get to be one of the family and bond with people. Certainly my favorite situation.

Wherever you are working, remember that our work is collaborative and that everyone is doing his best. Cut people some slack if they are less than charming. They may be as frightened as you.

Can't We All Just Get Along?

Actors are just like civilians, they love famous people and feel (rightly) that working with a famous person will give them more prestige. It certainly enhances a resume. Working with stars can be just as delightful (or not) as working with everyday people.

Stars frequently direct you. It never bothers me although it makes some other actors crazy. When I feel the idea is good, I use it. On occasion I have seen stars blatantly give an actor notes that will make his performance worse, so be sure to evaluate the advice before you take it. It does no good to resist, to go to the director or to get cranky about it. Just tell the star what a great idea it is, thank him profusely and do what you want.

I once worked with a well-known actress who must have been upset that the writers had given me a very powerful scene to play. The scene called for tears. As we started to shoot my scene, the actress managed to drop something, flub a line or otherwise ruin the scene over and over.

She assumed the more we did the scene, the less emotional juice I would have to expend. Too bad for her, that day, I was able to be extremely focused. The only thing she accomplished was to cost the producers more money because we had to shoot it so many times.

Some actors (stars or not) will purposely ruin a take if they do not like the way they looked in it. This keeps the director from making the decision to use the scene for someone else's good performance. There's not much you can do about that.

If you are working with a very competitive actor who feels he can only look good if you look bad, your only real defense is not to get hooked into it. I have heard stories of actors one-upping one another in this regard. Some actors are able to be quite powerful in offsetting this and consider it a testing of sorts and don't get all cranky about it. It can be disconcerting, but if you rise to the occasion, it can also be invigorating.

There are many stories about Marilyn Monroe and the filming of *Some Like it Hot*. She would supposedly not come out of her trailer until the afternoon. By that time, her co-stars had been waiting for her since morning. They were tired, frustrated, angry and no longer at their best. Billy Wilder supposedly told both Jack Lemon and Tony Curtis that they better be good all the time, because any take that Marilyn was good in, he was going to print.

Who knows if her tardiness was fear regarding her own performance or competition with her fellow actors?

My friend Leslie shot a TV movie in a small town in Pennsylvania. Much time had been spent rehearsing in New York before the company went on location so that when the day came to actually shoot, all the actors had to do was mark it for the camera one time and then shoot. Leslie's scene involved a verbal fight with a much more experienced actress. Leslie had all the lines while her opponent was to attempt to interrupt. As the director called *action* and the rehearsal began, the other actress slugged Leslie full in the face. The slap was an incredible stimulus for the scene and it played better than it had ever played. The only problem was that the camera was not rolling. Because no one had called *cut*, Leslie continued her performance at a high pitch and had nothing left when the camera was rolling. Whatever the motivation of the other actress, Leslie missed her own biggest moment in the film.

Professional Relationships

Networking is a dirty word to many of you, I know: *Oh, I'm not good at all that bullshit* or *I don't want to get a job just because I know someone* or *I'm here for art, not for commercialism,* etc., etc., etc.

Come on, wouldn't you really rather work someplace where you feel comfortable and with a director that you already know you can trust? Well, management feels the same way and it's their money that's on the line.

That being the case, keep up with directors, producers, writers and casting people you have worked with. And that doesn't mean just sending them a note when you are appearing in something, keep up with their careers and let them know when they do something you like. They know you're an actor and that you want a job, and if you're good, hiring you will only make them look good. So do your part, keep in touch and keep growing. Besides, when you become a star, you'll want to recommend directors as well as make-up people, costumers and the best of everyone you know and admire.

Many jobs in episodes are given to people who have worked with the director before — except for smaller roles, so do as much as you can to stay connected.

Keep meticulous notes. If you meet with a casting director and are able to find out that she has a 10-year-old daughter named Diane, then that information should go on a card to help you remember the casting director and to give you something to talk about. Not only will the casting director appreciate your effort, but you will be able to audition better for you will feel more comfortable. Life is about connecting, being in the moment, and treating people with respect. If you don't take the time to do that, it doesn't matter how many jobs you get, you'll continually feel that something is missing.

Practice connecting all the time. Talk to the

people in the grocery store or the people at the bank. Have conversations with everybody. Practice remembering and using their names. Find out something about them. Notice what makes one person different from another. Become a student of human nature. You'll not only become a better actor, but a more appealing person as well. The act of networking will simply be keeping up with your friends.

When my son was in graduate school, his major professor always made sure that when a visiting professor spoke on campus, the graduate students met for coffee afterwards with the star and conversed. He brought Dr. Smart to my son saying, *Dr. Smart, I want you to meet Jamie Callan, he is working on thus and such. Jamie, Dr. Smart is an authority on whatever.*

As a result, when Jamie (a Ph.D. himself, now) reads something that relates to Dr. Smart's project, he can drop that it in an envelope with a note saying that this material made him think of Smart and his project and *how it is going anyway?*

It's nice when someone sets up the guidelines for a conversation, but with a little imagination, you'll be able to do that for yourself. The key is to focus on the other person.

Facilitate

Another way of staying in touch with colleagues is by being a facilitator; helping other people. If a casting director is looking for a particular type, don't be afraid to mention the best actor you can think of for the project. Remember the names of producers and directors, costumers and set designers. Be happy to share a terrific person you have worked with and suggest how she might solve somebody else's problem. If you can't remember names, keep notes and use them. What goes around comes around.

Actors who have given up believing in fairytales in real life still have a hard time letting go as far as the business is concerned. Me, too. I know the score and I still believe the movies. I still think that if I got an Academy Award nomination it would change my career. In fact, it would change my social status. But even that is only during the time between when the nominations come out and the winner is announced. A win is good for a few more months, but not much more.

The Los Angeles Times addressed the Oscar issue in an interesting article entitled, *Is Oscar Nomination a Career Boost?* regarding the women nominees for best supporting actresses:

✦   *...ask the agents who represent these women about the impact of the nominations on their careers and it becomes clear that even the luster of an Academy of Motion Picture Arts and Sciences Oscar nomination doesn't alter a movie business truism:*

"As we all know," agent Susan Streitfeld lamented the other day, "to be in this business you should be 21 and beautiful."

Only Anne Archer, who plays younger than her 40 years and is drop-dead gorgeous in her nominated role as the good wife and mother in Fatal Attraction, *claims to be rolling in scripts. But Archer's situation is in sharp contrast to that of other nominees.*

Is Oscar Nomination a Career Boost?
Ellen Farley
Los Angeles Times
March 30, 1988

I have watched friends of mine win awards with varying results. The plain facts are that awards, by and large, are economic considerations that only incidentally benefit the actor. They were instituted originally to draw attention to the projects of the producers. Today the sponsors of such ceremonies use them not only to promote their industry, but to gain large television revenues for the awards ceremony.

A Tony is very prestigious within the Broadway theater community and will certainly get you considered for more parts. Two Tonys are worth a lot more than one and three are worth even more than that. They signify that you have become a bonafide member of the Broadway fraternity (notice that I did not say sorority, for it is still mainly a man's game). Employers in Los Angeles could not care less about Broadway awards unless the winners were in some huge international success that gained great media attention.

One Emmy was thrilling for a friend of mine. But it was only after the second win that she moved up to become a member of the hierarchy. She still finds herself unemployed sometimes and she still loses out to performers of more visibility but her status is forever changed and she can command more money.

The Academy Award is still the most prestigious award, but I can't remember who won last year, can you? I don't care, I still want one. I think winning an award would make most of us heady.

Because of the vast amount of television product, the members of the Television Academy can't possibly see everything and few take it seriously enough to vote only for those performances they see. I know all these things. Do you really think I will remember them if I'm ever nominated?

The whole awards process mostly puts actors in a cranky mood. When you spend your whole life thinking one of these events is going to change your standing in the business and it doesn't, it's disappointing. Actors tend to think, then, that all is lost. Nothing is any more lost than it was the day before.

You are not a better or worse actor because you were or were not nominated or did or did not win. Just think of it as your birthday. If you are lucky, on your birthday, people treat you very well. Then, the next day, it isn't your birthday. You are able to accept that and it's very similar.

Rags to Riches and Back Again

Henry Winkler had to hitchhike to the audition for *Happy Days*. He was, in fact, picked up by one of the people who ended up hiring him. Henry was young and made it big.

Danny DeVito and Rhea Perlman lived in a one room apartment for 15 years in New York before they began to work with any regularity for money.

As wonderful as it is to finally make it, it's just as depressing when casting directors and producers decide an actor is overexposed. The actor can then go from being a household name to being totally unemployed for years.

Howard Keel, who was a huge star 30 years ago on Broadway and in MGM musicals, told me an interesting story at a dinner party. When musicals went out of business, so did Keel and he spent years unemployed and depressed. He finally gave up and decided to move to Oklahoma City and get into the oil business. He considered himself a failure when he hired the truck and left California. In true Hollywood style, as soon as he had accepted his new lifestyle, a phone call came that put him back to work on the hit television series, *Dallas*.

One needs perspective on oneself and the business if he is to survive. The point of it all is to have the chance to work. Very few people get to pick and choose, even people as visible and successful as Jessica Tandy. This interview with Miss Tandy's husband, Hume Cronyn was written at the time of her death. I think it makes a good point:

✦ *"Jessie adores working," Mr. Cronyn said in 1986. "She's more fully alive when she's working." As she got older she seemed to be in ever greater demand, but over the years she took good parts and she took bad parts. "You are richer for doing things," she said. "If you wait for the perfect part or for what sends you, you will have long waits, and you will deteriorate. You can't be*

an actor without acting."
Jessica Tandy, a Patrician Star
of Theater and Film, Dies at 85
Marilyn Berger
The New York Times
September 12, 1994

Being Realistic About the Business

My own choice of acting was not based in any way on the reality of what the life is really about. Actually, it may have been based on what the life was about when I was five years old, but the business is totally different today than it was then.

It is even different today than it was in 1980. At that time, there was a long actors strike that had profound effects on the industry. Actually, I don't think the actors strike changed the business. The strike only reflected the changes that had already occurred in the industry and the world.

For whatever reason, since that time there has been much less product; there are far fewer jobs for everyone. Smaller parts that would have gone to actors with no name value are now taken by stars.

Parts on episodes once available to the working actor are now held back for actors who are already employed on nighttime series. The result is that for other than star film actors and actors regularly employed in very successful nighttime shows, it is more difficult than ever.

Series Stardom Forever — Not

The star and producer of one of the world's most popular shows found out the hard way that television stardom is unpredictable.

✦   *After his* Knight Rider *series was canceled by NBC in 1986, David Hasselhoff couldn't get a job. It didn't deter the brawny, six-foot, four-inch actor, who has repeatedly turned cancellations of series to his advantage. He's the first to admit that four years spent talking to a car, coupled with his good looks, only saddled him with the label "Can't Act."*

"It was a touchy time," he admits. "I couldn't get a job because I wasn't taken seriously after Knight Rider. *Scripts would call for a David Hasselhoff type, yet no one wanted the real thing. But when you think about it, I spent all that time talking to a car and I made it work. So there I was, sitting out on my back lawn thinking, Holy s--t! What am I going to do with all this energy?"*

> *Muscle Man*
> Kathleen O'Steen
> *Emmy*
> December 1995

Although he was lucky enough to get another show, *Baywatch*, that show was canceled after one year. Hasselhoff's entrepreneurial skills are what saved him. After producing his own record album and realizing he had enormous popularity internationally, David teamed up with the lifeguard who created the series and they have produced the show themselves to enormous success.

Just because Eriq LaSalle is a big star on *ER* didn't mean that all doors opened for him, either. As I mentioned in Chapter Two, Eriq truly understands that the only person you can count on in this business is yourself.

✦   *"When this show goes off the air in, let's say, five years, if I haven't done anything — and this is something minority artists really need to understand since we can't play by the same rules — if I'm not careful, I'm a forgotten entity. I could end up as this actor who used to be on this show. There are no guarantees [that] when this show is over I get to do a film."*

....after four years of trying unsuccessfully to sell a screenplay the conventional way — shopping it around through an agent — Eriq LaSalle thought he would try a more unorthodox approach.

LaSalle, a regular on the top-rated TV show, ER *took*

*out a $140,000 loan. He got help from Steven Spielberg, NBC
and Warner Brothers in securing equipment and filmed a 35-
minute version of* Psalms From the Underground. *LaSalle
wrote, directed and had a supporting role in the short film.*

Filmmaker With a Strong Pulse
Claudia Puig
The Los Angeles Times
November 18, 1995

After his film was screened, his script was sold to
Mel Gibson's Icon Productions with Eriq attached as director. More than anything else, LaSalle and Hasselhoff
have demonstrated that they are self-starters who have
the ability, courage and vision to not only take a chance,
but invest their own money and see a venture through to
conclusion. Those are the traits that make people in the
industry want to be in business with you.

What Have You Been Doing?

There's a wonderful joke about the actor who
was found in bed with another man's wife. The irate
husband demanded, *What have you been doing?*

The actor struck a pose, scratched his head and
recounted, *A recurring part in* NYPD Blue, *two shots on* Ally
McBeal *and a TV movie.*

Most of the time, when someone asks an actor
that question, they want to know, *Are you working as an
actor?* I'm instantly guilty when someone asks me the
question and I'm not working. It doesn't matter that I
might have written four books, gone to China,
volunteered at the hospital and saved four people from a
burning building. Nothing seems to count but working as
an actor.

I never ask if a friend has been working and I
never volunteer that information about myself. If one of
us has been working and the other one hasn't, it can be
uncomfortable. If it becomes apparent that we have both
been working or that we are both not working, then we

can discuss the business, but I'd rather talk about something else.

Civilians, of course, do not understand. When I lived in New York, I did a great many commercials, but like everyone else, I went through dry periods without much on the air. During a particularly depressing time, one of the people in my apartment building (whom I didn't know) greeted me warmly and said, *Say, haven't seen you on the tube lately. Have you left the business?*

No, I wanted to scream at him, *I feel like the business has left me.*

You are not paranoid. Your worst nightmares are true. If you are not currently working (visible), everyone concludes that you are dead and out of the business. Let this be their problem, don't buy into that thinking for yourself. You are neither dead nor out of the business. You are only out of work. You have been given a gift of time — to study, do your Christmas shopping or get married — before your next job. The way you choose to think about periods of not working will make a profound difference in your life.

There will be times (sometimes long times) when you will not work. If you choose to stay home and eat, sleep, cry, drink or do any of 100 other self destructive choices available, instead of making your own work and/or getting on with your life, you will be missing out on time that could be productive and happy.

In order to work it is true that you will have to be a detective to find the job and a press agent to capitalize on your good fortune. You must have the courage and nerve of a gambler to negotiate your contracts and also to take a chance doing something original at an audition. Only a gambler would stay in a business when it seems as though the odds are against you (and they always are).

You must constantly study to refine your craft; you must be an entrepreneur to create your own work, whether you become a book reviewer, a director, a producer, a teacher or stand-up or any of the other actor options within the field. You must have the character insights of a psychologist not only to break down a character, but to understand basic human behavior (yours as well as the person you are dealing with), and surely you will have to become a philosopher in order to put all this in a proper perspective.

If you are a smart actor, you will not allow success to stifle these gifts. Actors frequently believe that a measure of success brings freedom from the entrepreneurial aspects of the work. When we become concerned with protecting position and status and lose touch with our own action and vision, work frequently dries up.

Systems Dynamics Exchange

My son explained a useful engineering concept to me. It has to do with systems dynamics exchange. The principle can be demonstrated with my furnace. When I turn up the thermostat in my house, it takes a few minutes for the furnace to kick on. It takes even longer for my house to warm up. Therefore, if I'm smart, I will turn on the thermostat before I am cold. So it is with our careers, getting lazy frequently means getting left out in the cold.

Wrap Up

✓ there are many kinds of auditions
✓ prepare carefully
✓ choose material that suits you
✓ your behavior is important
✓ insecurity is unappealing
✓ wait intelligently
✓ learn about negotiation
✓ lots of us have been replaced
✓ it's important to get along with fellow actors
✓ getting hired depends on many factors
✓ being right can be more important than being good
✓ professional behavior is always noticed

- ✓ networking is important
- ✓ learn to be a facilitator
- ✓ deal with reality not your fantasies
- ✓ awards can change your status in the business — or not
- ✓ using the concept of systems dynamics exchange can help you stay employed

12 Agents/Managers

At the beginning of my career, I thought if I got the right theatrical agent, he could/would make me a star. I thought agents had the power of making or breaking your career. I knew this wasn't true in commercials because when I did commercials back home in Texas, I had learned how to call on film companies and advertising agencies myself. That meant I didn't feel so dependent on agents for this service since I had already been successful and had a reel of commercials to show. I felt I was at least employable.

Although I had no idea how a theatrical agent would receive me, my previous experience had taught me to be businesslike about calling on agents. I told myself I could not eat lunch until I had visited at least one theatrical agent. I would get myself up for it by telling myself if I did not go in and leave a picture and resume I had no chance. But if I left a picture and resume, the agent would be aware of my existence, at least, and my chances would improve.

But after all my late lunches, it was through a commercial agent that I got the break that gave me credibility with theatrical agents. Estelle Tepper (now a casting director in Los Angeles) was working in a New York talent agency that submits for both commercial and theatrical projects. One day, she had the opportunity to submit actors for a film entitled *The Gap*.

I'm pretty sure she must have emptied out her drawer and submitted every actor she had who was the right color and within 10 years of being the right age. Regardless, that is how Peter Boyle, Dennis Patrick, Audrey Caire and I came to be cast in a film that was listed on many 10 best lists for 1971. The movie, Susan Sarandon's first film, was released with a new title: *Joe*.

After the film and some very nice personal reviews, I still didn't choose an agent. In New York it's easy to exist working freelance and I was so frightened of choosing the wrong agent that I didn't choose one at all. Finally, the late Jay Wolfe, a wonderfully kind and talented casting director said, *K, you have to choose an agent. It just doesn't look good not to be signed.*

Though I now had the credits to attract an agent and had reached a place in the business where I needed an agent to maintain credibility, I still didn't know how to intelligently choose one.

Instead of educating myself, I chose a manager and gave away 15% more of my money (even on the commercial business built myself). Having a manager did not increase my business, so I finally gathered my courage, left the manager and chose a wonderful agent.

You Can't Be Passive & Successful at the Same Time

Respected Los Angeles acting teacher, Larry Moss says *You cannot be passive about your potential. You can't blame your agent. What you need is inside your self.*

Again, acting is not about being chosen. It has to be about the work. The actor must get fulfillment from the work. If you do what you love fully, in a concentrated and committed fashion, you already have your reward, no matter what. If you work to get chosen, you will have a more difficult time distilling your essence, you will burn yourself out constantly second guessing the marketplace and worse, you will be perpetually disappointed.

Although an agent is important, he can only sell a marketable product. That means that the actor must maintain his physical appearance, deal optimistically with unemployment and aging, and preserve his emotional health in an atmosphere that seems to thrive on pulling him down.

Even though I've been in the business over 30 years and I know all this, it's still a temptation to place too much emphasis on my agent. I want to believe he is getting, or not getting me, appointments. That way, when I'm not going out, it must be his responsibility.

It's not.

Successful Careers & Longevity

If you look in any analytical way at a successful person's career, you will see a body of work that is supported (by and large) by good mental and physical health, a strong sense of identity and self-confidence coupled with shrewd business savvy.

There are those few very young stars who luck into television series and films that can quickly make incredible stars that are so huge that you (and they) can't believe they will ever be out of work again. They will.

No one was bigger than Henry Winkler when he played The Fonz when *Happy Days* was the number one show on television. As important as that show was during its run, it was but a brief moment in Winkler's life and if he hadn't held onto his perspective and perfected other talents during his tenure of being hot, he could be sitting home today with all his *TV Guide* covers instead of directing and producing.

Credits Attract Agents

It's frustrating, but understandable, that credible agencies (who are not in the business of starting careers) don't want you until you have done the groundwork. Your ability to find a way into the business on some level demonstrates your employability and resourcefulness and makes you a credible business partner.

You must become so marketable that you are able to attract an agent whose contacts coupled with your growing reputation result in a job or an audition for one. The most successful agent in town can't sell a turkey. He might be able to force someone to take you, but why would he want to?

Since one of your goals is to attract an agent, you will want to consider what kind of actor excites them.

The Definitive Client

✦   *I want to know either that the actor works and makes a lot of money so that I can support my office or that the potential to make money is there. I am one of the people who goes for talent, so I do take people who are not big money makers, because I am impressed with talent.*

> Martin Gage, agent
> *The Gage Group*, Los Angeles

✦   *More jobs are available for certain types of actors than other types so you look at the physicality, for that look you know can sell. And nine times out of ten, that look is gorgeous. Men. Women. Beautiful. It's just a fact.*

> Ric Beddingfield, manager
> Los Angeles

✦   *I love a good resume. Even if there is no TV and film, if someone has great training and practical experience, even if it's La Mirada Steak House Dinner Theater, it's nice to see that. Some people make up video tapes with monologues on it. It's nice when an actor comes in well prepared. For example, if he's gotten key casting people to call me and networks his way into the office. I'm impressed with that.*

> Daryl Marshak, agent
> *Gold/Marshak and Associates*, Los Angeles

✦   *I want an actor with the ability to get a job and pay me a commission.*

> Beverly Anderson, agent
> *Beverly Anderson*, New York

✦   *My favorite kind of client? I like character actors. I like black actors and Hispanic actors very much. I understand them. I don't know why. We like developing people. We look at backgrounds. I like stage. I love people who do the footwork. When I see a blank resume and they say, 'I'm talented, trust me,' that's the kiss of death in this office. I can see when someone has gone through the theater department; someone has done a lot of Equity Waiver plays. I appreciate that. When someone tells me they study a lot, that kind of scares me. I think there's studying and there's practical experience.*

Daryl Marshak, agent
Gold/Marshak & Associates, Los Angeles

♦ *If they're a character actor, you have to ask yourself, "Do I need another character actor in my life?" Or, if they're attractive, then you have to start praying they can act.*

Ric Beddingfield, manager
Los Angeles

New York agent Beverly Anderson told me about meeting a prospective client:

♦ *Sigourney Weaver asked to come in and meet me when she was with a client of mine in Ingrid Bergman's show,* The Constant Wife. *She's almost six feet tall. I'm very tall myself and when I saw her, I thought, 'God, honey, you're going to have a tough time in this business because you're so huge.'*

And she floated in and she did something no one had ever done. She had this big book with all her pictures from Bryn Mawr or Radcliffe of things she had done and she opened this book and she comes around and drapes herself over my shoulders from behind and points to herself in these pictures. She was hovering over me. And I thought no matter what happens with me, this woman is going to make it. There was determination and strength and self-confidence and positiveness. Nobody's ever done that to me before.

Beverly Anderson
Beverly Anderson, New York

♦ *Training is the most important thing. I get very annoyed with people. Someone is attractive, so people say, 'You should be in television', and then the actor thinks that's going to just happen.*

J. Michael Bloom, agent
J. Michael Bloom and Associates/Los Angeles

So, agents are looking for:

- training
- experience
- talent
- looks
- potential
- commerciality
- presence
- attitude
- self-confidence
- competitiveness

Well, I'd like to find all those things in an agent.

The Definitive Agent

If Beverly Anderson looks mainly for an actor who can get the job, I think the actor has to be primarily looking for an agent who can get him the audition. That sounds pretty simple, doesn't it?

Well, if the actor/agent relationship were based on getting auditions for everything, then the agent would have a right to say that you must get everything he sends you out on.

Getting an audition isn't necessarily the most important thing, either. Is he sending you on the right auditions? Does he see you accurately? Do you both have the same perception regarding the roles you are right for?

The agent has to know what the actor can do, what the range is so he knows how to handle that particular artist.

Jeff Berg is the chairman of one of the business' most important and powerful agencies, International Creative Management (ICM), which represents clients like Anthony Hopkins, Tommy Lee Jones and Holly Hunter. He makes some good points about agents:

✦   *I'll tell you what I like about agents. I like the fact that*

agents look to make it happen. And a good agent can't take 'no'
and expect to support himself. Agents have to develop a kind of
resistance to rejection, and I think it makes you stronger and I
think it makes you better.

> *Hollywood's No. 2 Agent Views His Status*
> *and His World, Philosophically*
> Bernard Weinraub
> *The New York Times*
> March 2, 1994

I asked other agents what qualities they would
look for if they were choosing agents. They mentioned
integrity, client list, communication, background and
taste.

To know whether an agent possesses these traits,
you'll have to do some research. *Reel Power*, written by
Mark Litwak and published by William Morrow, is a
good place to start.

✦ *One of the chief factors that determines the value of an*
agent is information. It is impossible for a small agent to possess the
amount of information that a large agent can. We track hundreds
of projects weekly at all of the studios and networks. If a client
walks in and asks about a project, I can haul out 400 pages of
notes and say, "Oh yeah, its at this studio and this is the producer
and they're doing a rewrite right now and they're hoping to go with
it on this date and talking to so-and-so about it." I have that
information.

> *Gene Parseghian*, agent
> *The William Morris Agency*, Los Angeles

So, Gene thinks (and I certainly agree) that
information is important. Two other traits I want in an
agent are:

Access and Stature

The dictionary defines access as *ability to approach*
or *admittance.* Conglomerate agencies have so many stars

on their lists, they have plenty of *ability to approach*. If the studios, networks and producers do not return their phone calls, they might find the agency retaliating by withholding their important stars.

Stature, on the other hand, is entirely different. Webster defines the word as *level of achievement*. So, other prestigious, mid-level agents like J. Michael Bloom and Martin Gage surely have more stature than some lowly agent at William Morris, but possibly not as much access.

There's also the question of style. I know an actor who had a very effective agent who yelled at everyone (the client and the casting directors). That's not to say the agent didn't get the actor appointments, he did. The actor simply decided that wasn't the way he wanted to be represented, so he left.

In smaller marketplaces, the same qualifiers hold true. There may just be one agent in town for you to choose from, who may not have stature and/or access. Then you will have to acquire these attributes yourself. It's not impossible. We (and they) build credibility by telling the truth. By saying something and carrying through. Don't promise something you can't deliver. If you can get someone to see you and experience you and you have something to sell, they will hire you. Perhaps not today, but it will happen.

Size

When you are shopping for an agent, make sure you get one that is your size. The most effective formula is the agency with the smallest number of credible clients and the largest number of well-respected agents. Many agents believe a good ratio is one agent to 20-25 actors.

For a successful partnership, you and your agent must have the same goals and visions. If you think you can be a star and your agent doesn't or if he sees you as a star and you want a different kind of career, you're both going to be frustrated and the relationship won't work. Aggressiveness and enthusiasm are part of the mix as well as integrity. In a fairytale business, it's comforting and necessary to know that at least one person is telling you the truth.

So the chief factors to look for in an agent are:

- stature and access
- shared career vision
- enthusiasm
- aggressiveness
- actor/agents ratio
- compatibility
- style
- integrity

Let's say you have now landed the agent of your dreams (or the only agent in town). Now what?

The Relationship

All relationships take time, thought, creative energy and communication in order to bond and be successful. This includes your partnership with your agent. As in other unions, it is important to know what you want from the alliance in order to get it. It is better to decide what you require before you sign a contract. What do you need from your agent in order to feel not only well represented, but comfortable? There's a whole list of things I need.

It's important to me that my agent return my phone calls promptly. That might not be important to someone else, but it is high on my list of requirements.

I also want my agent to submit me for any job I am right for. I would like him to have the stature to get his phone calls returned from important casting directors and producers.

I want him to have the imagination and aggressiveness to suggest me for roles that might be terrific for me, though unusual casting-wise.

I think we all want to be able to communicate

honestly and easily with our agent, but trust doesn't happen in a day, from either one of you. There is going to be a period of getting acquainted and learning each other's signals. Don't be impatient. This person is your business partner. He needs to talk to you as much as you need to talk to him if he is going to represent you well.

Your agent doesn't have to be involved in your social circle, but he can be. Some people want their agents to console them when they're not working. If that is your need and your arrangement, fine, but it's really not part of the job description.

It's important to know what you want and to communicate that information to your prospective business partner as well to find out what his needs are in order to negotiate the shape of your prospective partnership. It's going to be a marriage, after all, so you will need to have the same goals, tastes, value system and vision regarding the possibilities of your union.

Getting Started

The best way to contact an agent is through a referral. If you know someone on the agent's list who can act as a go-between, that is fine.

If you know a casting director you have worked with well enough, you might ask him for advice about agents to contact and see if the casting director volunteers to make a call for you, but what if you don't have that entree?

If you are young and beautiful, drop your picture off looking as y&b as possible. If you are really y&b and can speak at all, few will require you do much more. It's sad (for the rest of us), but true, so you may as well cash in on it. If you are smart, you will study while cashing in. Y&B doesn't linger long and you may want to work during those grey years of your 30's and beyond.

As I mentioned earlier, I think it's best to send a letter a couple of days before sending a picture and resume. Letters get read while pictures and resumes tend to sit in the *as soon as I get to it* stack. Address your letter to a specific agent, preferably one of the associates. They get less mail than the owner so you might get attention much sooner.

Remember, type your letter and use good paper. State that you are looking for representation and that you are impressed with the agency's client list (make sure you know who is on it) and that your credits compare favorably. Tell them your picture and resume will arrive in the next day's mail.

Make sure they do. Do not say you want this person for your agent (you don't know that yet). Mention a few key credits. If your credits don't look that impressive, but you did work with Martin Scorcese and Stephen Spielberg, by all means note that. If your letter has piqued interest, your picture will be opened immediately.

Mail your letter so that it arrives on Wednesday or Thursday away from the first of the week rush. On Monday, not only is the agent catching up from the weekend, many actors have been doing their homework over the weekend and have sent their pictures, so the agent's desk is full. If your letter arrives later in the week, it will have less competition.

Your follow-up call (late afternoon is the best time) should be brief and upbeat. Be a person the agent wants to talk to. If he doesn't want a meeting, get over the disappointment and go on to the next agent on your list.

When Carol Burnett went to New York, agents said to call when she was in something. Didn't they know if she was in something that she wouldn't need an agent?

Finally, she enlisted her boyfriend (a writer) and the young women she lived with in a residence for young actresses. They produced their own show and invited all the agents in town. They all came!

When I interviewed New York agent Lionel Larner, (Glenda Jackson and Carroll O'Connor are just two of his famous clients) he told me: *Tell actors to produce something in their living room and invite agents. I would come.*

There really is an agent for everyone no matter where you live. Your focus, energy and attitude can put you ahead of the pack. If you are committed, shoulder your responsibilities, do the work and pursue employment in a professional manner, you will prosper.

Audition Tape

If you're not appearing at some venue where an agent can see you work, you really need an audition reel. Compile a tape (no longer than eight minutes) as soon as you have any professional examples of your work. When you are just beginning, this might be several commercials (or moments from the commercials that feature you), a student film or even a non-union film. It can be two minutes or five, it doesn't have to be eight, but it should be something to show what you look like on film and give some idea of your range. This is a quick sales tool that can save you and the agent a lot of time.

A few years ago I received a frantic call from a woman who explained to me that she was enrolled in a seminar I was teaching that weekend for the American Film Institute, but that she needed me sooner. She had an appointment with an agent on Friday and she wanted to know if she could make an appointment for a consultation.

I told her to bring everything she had. Pictures, resumes, any examples of her work on film. She was about 35, overweight, blowzy, very nice. I looked at her film and suggested that she *not* go to the agent without a reel. We selected the scenes we felt were best and she rushed to have a tape made.

A week later, she called to tell me that when she got to the agent's office, the agent seemed unimpressed and passed her off to her assistant. The actress left her tape anyway. Over the weekend, she discovered another piece of film that she wanted to add to her tape. She called the agent's office to see if they had looked at the tape. They hadn't gotten to it yet and were annoyed that she had called. She explained that she had more film to add to it and that she would like to come by, pick it up, add the tape and return. There was a lot of sighing: *All right. Come and get it.*

By the time the actress got there, the agent had looked at the tape. She was welcomed warmly: *Come in. Come in. We think you are wonderful. Can we sign you?*

Without the tape, she would probably have been passed over. It is pretty impossible to tell in an office meeting whether or not you are a good actor or to have any idea of someone's range.

Producing a tape of yourself is often a waste of money because most agents either will not look at a home produced tape or will not give it much credibility. Therefore, one of your first goals should be to amass professional work on film. Call every theater and film school in your area and volunteer for student films. Do what you can with commercials and Industrial Film. This is an important entree into the business.

The Meeting

Okay, you've got an appointment. Now what will you do? How will you dress? How will you behave? What question should you ask?

Although you are there to present yourself to the agent, he is the salesman, after all, so don't tell him he could make a lot of money on you. Agents have told me such self-serving remarks automatically conclude the meeting. He's not the agent for you if he can't figure that out by your presence and credits.

This is the time for clarity. Tell him you think you are due for a series, a film or whatever, but be realistic. Ask what he thinks is your next step; tell him what you think your strong points are.

Learn how the office works. If you're being interviewed by the owner, is he going to work for you or is he just the charmer? I know actors who signed with agencies because they were impressed with the owner, but after becoming his client, he rarely crossed the actor's path.

Can you drop by the office? Should you call first? Will the agents come to see your work? Will they consult with you before they turn down work? Are they good about returning phone calls? Explore your own feelings about these issues before you arrive.

If you need to be able to talk regularly to your agent, now's the time to mention it. He needs to know that's one of the things you require. You might want to ask if the office has a policy of regularly requesting audition material for clients at least a day in advance of the audition. Let him know your requirements to present yourself at your best. If that turns him off, this isn't the agent for you.

Isn't it nice to know there are specific things on your mind to ask about during the meeting so you won't just sit there quaking and hoping to be chosen?

Remembering how overeager people turn you off may help your perspective in these meetings. Remember, what you don't ask today can come back to haunt you tomorrow.

So, you were on time. You did not arrive with an unattractive attitude. You met. You asked questions. You were respectful. You have acted naturally. Now, be the one to end the meeting. Make it clear that you value the agent's time and view it as a precious commodity. He will appreciate that. Suggest you both think about the meeting for a day or two and then decide.

Be definite about when you will get back to him (it should be less than a week). You may have other agents to meet. Mention this. If he's last on the list, mention you have to go home and digest all the meetings.

Then go home and do just that. Let him know you were pleased with the meeting. Even if it wasn't your finest moment, or his, be gracious. After all, you both did your best.

Reality Check

I advise a 24-hour fantasy-shakedown period.
When I interviewed agents for my Los Angeles and New
York agent books, I wanted every agent I talked to while
I was with them. They are salesmen, after all. After a
cooling-off period, I found my feelings to be more
realistic. The hyperbole seemed to drift out of my head
and I was able to assess reality more clearly.

It is important to jot down your feelings and
thoughts about each meeting as soon as you get home.
Then, look at all the notes the next day and reevaluate
your appraisal. Never forget you are choosing an agent.
The qualities you look for in a friend are not necessarily
the same qualities you desire in an agent.

Now you are ready to digest all your research and
make a decision. You've done the hard part.

I heard a story about director, Mike Nichols. He
was giving a speech to the actors on opening night:

✦ *Just go out there and have a good time. Don't let it worry
you that* The New York Times *is out there; that every
important media person in the world is watching you; that we've
worked for days and weeks and months on this production; that the
investors are going to lose their houses if it doesn't go well; that the
writer will commit suicide and that this could be the end of your
careers if you make one misstep. Just go out there and have a good
time.*

I think this is the way many of us feel about
choosing an agent. We act as if it is a momentous
decision having irrevocable consequences on our careers.
It's not. You can get a job without an agent. An agent
can't book a job without an actor. Keep things in
perspective. Do the research, weigh the evidence, then
make the decision. The successful career is built on self-
knowledge.

Trust your instincts. You already know what to
do. Do it.

The Partnership

Once you have chosen the agent, visit him to sign contracts and meet (and fix in your mind) all the people in your new office. If there are several, note who is who and where they sit, as soon as you leave the office. Until you become more familiar with everyone, you can consult your map before each subsequent visit.

Leave a good supply of pictures and resumes. If you have videocassette tapes, leave those, too, as well as a list of casting directors, producers and directors with whom you have relationships. Alphabetize the list if you ever want the agent to use it. Keep abreast of current productions so that the next time Steven Spielberg has a project, you can remind your agent that you and Steven went to school together. After all, your agent has lots of clients.

Also leave a list of your quotes (how much you were paid for your last jobs in theater, film and television), plus information on billing. The more background you give your agent, the better he can represent you. If it's a large office, leave each agent your quotes and contacts.

90%/10%

Now the real work begins. Remember the agent only gets 10% of the money. You can't really expect him to do 100% of the work.

It's time for you to focus on your expectations. If you don't want him to be lazy, set a good example. Let him see how hard you are working to perfect and sell yourself. Let him see how enthusiastic you are. He will take his cue from you.

It's similar to one's relationship to one's children. If you have a positive view of life and act on it, the chances are that your children will, also. If your children see you taking care of business, that's the norm. How you and your agent function together is a joint work in progress to which you will both contribute. I don't want to suggest that you can reform anyone's character. I'm assuming that with your diligence and investigation, you have already chosen a like-minded agent.

We hope agents are going to initiate work for us and introduce us to casting directors, producers, directors, etc., but their real contribution over a career span is negotiating, making appointments for us, being supportive in our dark moments and helping us retain our perspective in the bright moments.

Give a good agent a real career to work with and watch him build the momentum. Even then, successful actors don't just hand it all over. They continue to do 90% of the work.

What Does That Mean?

Your agent's job is to get the buyer enthusiastic about you. Your job once you get an agent is to keep your agent enthusiastic about you.

When I finally signed with an agent in New York, after successfully freelancing for a long time, I thought my part of the hustling was over. When I consider how much I might have contributed to my career if I had agented more, I'm pretty startled. My brain could have been teeming with all kinds of possibilities if I had even begun to think this way. It never even occurred to me that my agent might forget about me.

Consider this. If someone came into the room right now, gave you a script to read and then asked for your casting suggestions, who would you be able to think of? My bet is the list would be heavy with the actors you have just seen in a movie, on television, stage or in person. Is your agent any different?

Actor's Responsibilities

I know actors who are angry when they have to tell their agents how to negotiate for them. They feel the agent is not doing his job if he has to be reminded to go for a particular kind of billing or per diem or whatever. If the agent has it all together and does everything perfect, that's great, but it's your career. It's up to you to know what the union minimums are, how you go about getting more money and who else might be getting it. You are getting the 90%.

Not only is it your responsibility to have your own plan for your career, it's a way for you to be in control of your destiny in a business where it is all too easy to feel tossed about by fate.

It's your vision and your focus that have gotten the agent's interest in the first place. Why would you want to hand over your business to someone else? The larger the support system and the more sources of energy focusing on a single goal, the larger the payoff. You can't afford to give up your part in evaluating and guiding your career.

If you are looking for an agent in the Los Angeles or New York area, *The New York Agent Book* and *The Los Angeles Agent Book* detail agents, their background, clients and agency information. These books also discuss how to go about having relationships with agents.

When It Makes Sense to Have a Manager

Managers are a definite plus for child actors (see Chapter 9) who need guidance and whose families have no show business background. A manager usually places the child with an agent, monitors auditions and sometimes even accompanies the child to meetings.

If you are entering the business and need someone to help you with pictures, resumes, image, etc., managers can be helpful. There are, however, many agents who delight in starting new talent and consider this part of their service.

When you are at a big agency and it's too intimidating and time consuming to keep in touch with 20 agents, it might be advantageous to have a connected manager in your corner.

Changing agents is easier when you have a manager, because the manager does all the research, calling and rejection of the former agent, so sometimes actors choose managers primarily for this reason. It's an expensive way to avoid discomfort. If the manager doesn't work out, you'll only have to go through the unpleasantness when you decide you can handle your own business after all.

If you have the credits to support getting a good agent, you can do that on your own. If you don't, the manager can't create them.

I have a few friends who feel the presence of a manager enhanced their careers. One in particular said that when her agents were considering dropping her, that she and the manager read *The Breakdown* (see glossary) together, decided what she should be submitted for and she delivered her picture and resume to the casting office. If the manager got a call for an appointment, the actress went in and if she got the job, they called the agent to make the deal.

The agent became more enthusiastic about the actress for a while, but ultimately dropped her. The agent's earlier disinterest signaled what he had already decided: that she was no longer appropriate for their list. In that case, the manager, though helpful, only delayed the inevitable.

Changes in the Business

During the past several years, the role of managers has taken on a new color. With increasing regularity, many agents are closing their door as agents on Friday, and opening on Monday as managers, functioning largely the same, charging more (at least 15%) and freed of all those pesky Screen Actors Guild rules and regulations which protect the talent.

Mike Ovitz, after playing a major role in creating what was for a time the most important talent agency in the world (CAA), and following unsatisfying stints at Disney and Livent, is now, apparently getting back into the agency business but calling himself a manager:

✦ *Martin Scorcese and Barry Levinson have signed with Artists Management Group — the new management-production banner formed by Michael Ovitz, Rick Yorn and Julie Silverman-Yorn.*

...AMG, which has been in business for only a week, is understood to have signed several major clients.

Helmers join Ovitz at AMG
Chris Petrikin
Daily Variety
January 11, 1999

Ovitz' re-entry into the agenting business as a manager may end up causing the very regulations these new businesses are trying to avoid:

✦ *Sheila Kuehl, D-Encino, chair of the state Assembly's Judiciary Committee, said she will introduce a bill in February that should clarify the roles of managers and agents.*

...Kuehl said the bill would do two things: "One is to establish a new section in the law regulating artists' managers, in the same way that talent agencies are now regulated," she said. "The second thing it would do would be to make clear that only a talent agent can attempt to procure employment for an artist. There was nothing about managers in the law, so in this new section, it clearly says that only agents can attempt to procure employment..

"Managers would have to be licensed," she added, "post a bond and submit fingerprints and character affidavits. There would be a hearing to get the license, and it would have to be renewed every so often."

The Great CAA-Ovitz War:
Whose Side Are You On?
Stephen Galloway & David Robb
The Hollywood Reporter
January 27, 1999

Although there are many important, effective and

honest managers, there are many who are not. Agents must be franchised by the entertainment unions and the state, displaying at least a modicum of track record, honesty and skills before they are certified. There is no certifying group overseeing the activity or contracts of managers.

There is an association of personal managers, but many do not belong. Managers can charge whatever they can get away with and they can tie you up for years. When Eddie Murphy became successful, an enterprising manager appeared from his past claiming part of the spoils. He had a valid contract. I don't know what Murphy ended up paying, but the aggravation and court costs were not inconsiderable.

Although legislation is in the works to regulate managers much as agents are regulated, the managers are mounting a campaign to stop it. Regardless of their efforts, at some future point, they will have to follow some rules. Until that time, be careful.

Wrap Up

Agents

✓   self-agenting is always necessary
✓   strive to be the definitive client
✓   strive to get the definitive agent
✓   put together a good audition tape
✓   it's a relationship
✓   know your requirements
✓   be courageous about communicating
✓   get a meeting
✓   know what you are going to say
✓   remember that you're getting 90% of the money
✓   shoulder your responsibilities

Managers

✓ can provide access
✓ can provide guidance
✓ can be expensive
✓ are not governed by standard industry contracts
✓ be careful

13   Unions

When I was an aspiring actor, my goal was to join Actors' Equity, the only actors' union name I had ever heard of when I was in Texas dreaming of becoming an actress. I became a member of the Screen Actors Guild, but somehow I didn't feel like I was a real actor until I got into Equity. I wasn't any different from the day before, but I *felt* different and that is worth a lot; just like the Cowardly Lion getting courage with a medal in the *Wizard of Oz*.

One's goals and image of oneself aside, it is not always a good idea to join a union until you really have to. As I mentioned in Chapter 2, there is so much unemployment among all the actors who are already members of Screen Actors Guild that to presume that just showing up with a card is going to change things, is merely wishful thinking.

If you are not a member of the union, at least all those more experienced actors with better credits are not your competition. There are many non-union jobs available that might net you some work. Since the pay is low or non-existent, those out of work union actors (who have already done the groundwork you are now involved in) are not available for that work.

Non-union jobs include not only features with no union connection, but films for student filmmakers (they may be at regular colleges or in prestigious film schools like the American Film Institute, The University of Southern California, The New York Film School, etc.), or documentaries, government and educational films.

Investigate the project to see if it is worthwhile, but even a bad film will teach you a lot. You will see yourself on film, be on a set, watch set-ups and learn to get along with people in unpleasant and stressful situations. Use discretion; Traci Lords aside, sleezo film will not enhance your repertoire.

All the performer unions are members of an

alliance called the Association of Actors and Artists of America or the Four A's.

Once you are a member of any actors' union, you are not allowed to work in a non-union venture involved in the jurisdiction of any of the Four A's *if* that union is actively involved in bringing that production under union auspices.

So, if you are a member of SAG, but not Equity and Equity is trying to get a theater to become union affiliated, you cannot legally work in that project even though you are not a member of Equity. This circumstance doesn't happen very often. The concept is confusing, so if you are in a situation where you are not sure, check with your union before signing any contract; otherwise, you could be fined and brought up on charges.

The Los Angeles trade paper that lists casting news is *Backstage West*. The New York counterparts are *Backstage* and *Show Business*. In other marketplaces, check any university or school where students are involved in film. Read the classifieds. Be alert. Keep the word out when you are in theater circles that you are looking for opportunities.

Union Jurisdictions

Actors' Equity Association (AEA/Equity), founded in 1913, is the labor union representing actors and stage managers in the legitimate theater in the United States. Equity negotiates minimum wages and working conditions, administers contracts, and enforces the provisions of its various agreements with theatrical employers. There are currently about 40,000 active Equity members.

The American Federation of Television and Radio Artists (AFTRA), represents its members in four major areas: news and broadcasting; the recording business; entertainment programming; and commercials and non-broadcast, industrial, educational media.

AFTRA's 80,000 members are seen or heard on television, radio and sound recordings and include actors, announcers, news broadcasters, singers (including royalty artists and background singers), dancers, sportscasters, disc jockeys, talk show hosts and others. Talent payments under AFTRA contracts are over $1 billion a year. (This information from AFTRA's webpage: http://www.aftra.org/)

Screen Actors Guild (SAG) currently has over 90,000 members including the extras. In addition to filmed television shows and feature films, SAG also has jurisdiction over: Interactive multimedia, Infomercials, Low-budget films, Student films, Narration/voice-overs, Foreign film dubbing, Music videos, Experimental films, Singer sessions, Commercial demos, ADR (automated dialogue replacement), PSAs (public service announcements) Industrials/corporate videos, Dubbing promos and trailers and Made-for-video productions.

Union Membership Requirements

AEA (Actors' Equity Association) — Currently, Equity's initiation fee is $800. There are also Basic Dues of $78 per year, payable semi-annually in May and in November, and a 2% Working Dues deduction from a member's gross weekly earnings when employed under Equity contract. (Gross weekly earnings don't include the minimum portion of out-of-town or per diem expense monies.) The maximum Equity earnings subject to the 2% Working Dues is $150,000 a year.

Full membership privileges, including the right to vote, commence upon the signing of an application and the payment, within six months, of at least $300 of the initiation fee. Equity maintains a dues check-off system when performers are employed under an Equity contract that provides for the regular weekly deduction of any outstanding dues and initiation fees.

If a performer is not working under Equity contract, any outstanding balance due on the initiation fee must be paid not later than the second anniversary date of the membership application signing.

Both membership status and any monies previously paid are forfeited should a performer fail to complete payment of the full $800 initiation fee within this two-year maximum time period.

Rules for membership state you must have a verifiable Equity Contract in order to join or have been a member in good standing for at least one year in AFTRA or SAG. Check Equity's webpage for most current data: http://www.actorsequity.org.

AFTRA (American Federation of Television and Radio Artists) — New members must pay a one time initiation fee of $1,000 plus $42.50 covering the first dues period. Dues are billed each May 1st and November 1st and are based on a member's AFTRA earnings in the previous year.

Requirements for membership are lenient in AFTRA and seem to be based on having the money to pay the enrollment fee.

As previously mentioned, it can be a hindrance to join unions before you are ready as that puts you out of the running to do non-union films, shows, etc., and begin to amass film on yourself, so be patient.

For the most up-to-the-minute information about dues and benefits check out AFTRA's webpage at http://www.aftra.org.

SAG (Screen Actors Guild) — The most powerful actor's union is SAG. Performers may join upon proof of employment or prospective employment within two weeks or less by a SAG signatory company. Employment must be in a principal or speaking role in a SAG film, videotape, television program or commercial. Proof of such employment may be in the form of a signed contract, a payroll check or check stub, or a letter from the company (on company letterhead stationery). The document proving employment must provide the following information: applicant's name and Social Security number, the name of the production or the commercial (the product name), the salary paid in dollar amount, and the specific date(s) worked.

Performers may join SAG if the applicant is a

paid up member of an affiliated performers' union (AFTRA, AEA, AGVA, AGMA or ACTRA) for a period of at least one year and has worked at least once as a principal performer in that union's jurisdiction.

The Screen Actors Guild Initiation Fee as of 11-1-98 is $1,194.50. This seems like a lot of money (and is) but the formula involved makes some sense. It is SAG minimum, $576 for two days' work, which comes to $1,152, plus the first semiannual dues, $42.50.

This money is payable in full, in cashier's check or money order, at the time of application. The fees may be lower in some branch areas. SAG dues are based on SAG earnings and are billed twice a year. Those members earning more than $5,000 annually under SAG contracts will pay 1½% of all money earned in excess of $5,000 up to a maximum of $150,000.

Members who are paying full dues to another performers' union and earn less than $25,000 per year under SAG contracts will receive a reduction of $10 per year. Members whose SAG earnings exceed $25,000 per year will pay full dues, regardless of other guild affiliations.

All unions have Honorary Withdrawal status for members who are not working. HW relieves you of the obligation to pay your dues, but you are still in the union and prohibited from accepting non-union work.

Union Minimums

Equity Minimum — There are 18 basic contracts ranging from the low end of the Small Production Contract (from $100 to $390 weekly depending on the size of the theater) to the higher Production Contract covering Broadway houses, Jones Beach, tours, etc. ($1,000 weekly). Highest is the Business Theater Agreement, for shows produced by large corporations ($1,200 weekly).

AFTRA Minimum — The minimum contract as of 7-1-98 is $576 a day for prime time dramatic programs

on ABC, CBS or NBC. That rate increases by $20 after
7-1-99. There is a three-day rate of $1,457 which
increases to $1,508. The weekly rate of $2,000 will
increases to $2,070. AFTRA has differing rate categories
for daytime, announcers, newscasters, singers, chorus,
radio, voice over news and so on. Either check out the
webpage for more details or request a rate booklet from
AFTRA.

Since AFTRA's pay scale is so complicated (and
low), management often plays one union off against the
other. The fees I am quoting are for nighttime straight
on-camera acting.

Screen Actors Guild Minimum — SAG minimums
are on a parity with AFTRA: as of 7-1-98, SAG scale
rates require $576 daily and $2,000 weekly as a minimum
for employment in films and television. The fees will
escalate after 7-1-99 to $596 daily and $2,070 weekly.
Overtime in SAG is considerably higher than in
AFTRA.

Union initiation fees of the unions are expensive.
So, wait until you have a reasonable expectation of
actually working before joining.

Union Function

When you are ready to join the union, you are
joining a group with a courageous legacy:

✦   *It took a lot of courage to join a union in the anti-labor
climate of Hollywood in the thirties — especially a union for motion
picture performers. Actors' Equity made an unsuccessful attempt to
organize the field in 1928-9, so when a ragtag group of theater-
trained actors began a whispering campaign at a private men's club
known as The Masquers in 1933, it was an uphill battle. They
had to use passwords, backdoors, and secret alleyways to elude
studio detectives. The group's goal: to correct the abuses heaped upon
freelance players and to negotiate a square deal with fair wages and
working conditions for all performers.*

With American Federation of Labor recognition in

1935, the organization became an affiliated union, but it wasn't until mid-1937 when the studios accepted SAG's jurisdiction, that suddenly every actor had to join.

The Founding Members
Harry Medved
Screen Actor Sixtieth Anniversary Issue
1995

The unions fill an important need for actors. Powerless in many situations, actors are at least protected in the areas of basic working conditions. The unions provide hospitalization for members, keep track of residuals and are helpful when an actor has any kind of problem, particularly financial. There are loans and grants available to members in time of need. In addition, SAG, Equity, and AFTRA all are participating in a work program to help non-working members educate themselves to change careers if they are interested.

Every Family Has Its Problems

As in any large collective of disparate parts, there is frequently a great deal of grousing from members regarding their unions. SAG members have considerable internal dissension and the union threatens to break apart from time to time.

Equity was embroiled in disputes over casting in the Broadway hit, *Miss Saigon*. Those disputes were not only with the employers, but were a source of strife between members of the union.

AFTRA and SAG faced a hard decision when they voted jointly to establish jurisdiction over extras. Now that the extras are in SAG and AFTRA, there is constant conflict between the extra and the principal performers because their needs are different.

It's easy to take your unions for granted and bad mouth them when something doesn't go your way and you have not bothered to get the facts. This occurs particularly if you are not working and need a place to put all your anger and blame.

Some union members stab themselves in the back by working non-union jobs, hoping that the union will never find out. Sometimes union members work non-union unknowingly because they have not checked to see if the employer is a signatory to a basic contract with the union. Just because there is a major advertising agency or a visible star involved doesn't necessarily mean the job is union sanctioned.

Be diligent, for the union rules are very clear: a union member is not allowed financial gain from a non-union job. The union will bring you up on charges and fine you the amount of money you made on the job even if you thought the job was within the jurisdiction of the union. Therefore, it pays to make a simple phone call.

It is the actor's responsibility to call the union and find out if the producers have in fact signed an agreement with the union. Stationery stores sell blank Screen Actors Guild contracts, so just because you sign a form that says Screen Actors Guild, and the employer pays SAG rates, doesn't mean there is an agreement in force.

When you work a non-union job, there is no protection of basic working conditions, no contributions to health and welfare on the actors behalf (and therefore no hospitalization) and no guarantee of payment. When a producer makes an agreement with the unions, he puts up a bond guaranteeing the actor's salary.

Hospitalization, decent pay, residuals, guaranteed meal times and overtime compensation have all been won from employers over a long period of time through difficult negotiations. If you give these things away, you undermine your union and your own collective bargaining agreements.

Last but not least, *Daily Variety* reviews almost every film made, listing the names of all the actors involved; so, the union will most likely find out if you work non-union and you will be brought up on charges, possibly put on probation, fined and/or excluded from the union. You may well work under an assumed name,

but your face is still on the screen. You will be found out.
I know you want to work, but it's really not worth it.

If you are not far along enough in your career to
hold out for union jobs, don't join the union. If you are a
professional, act like one. Live up to your responsibility
by checking the status of projects you are considering.

Be Part of the Solution

Regardless of your union affiliation and
jurisdiction, become an asset to your group. Too many of
us become busy working and never take the time to go to
meetings, become informed regarding the issues, join
committees and become part of the policy making team.
This frequently leaves the rule making power to people
who are not working the contracts they are negotiating.
They are looking for ways to fill their time and although
they have good intentions, they are making rules they will
not be bound by; you will. Unless you are willing to
spend some time contributing, you have no right to
complain.

When you join, become active. Read the liter-
ature and become aware of the issues. Know what
minimum is. Know what isn't working in your current
contract. Form an idea about what would make things
better, then go to a meeting or write a letter and work to
put those plans into action.

Besides joining your union, align yourself with
any other local professional organization of actors. There
are groups of actors in every city who are looking for
other actors to work with. Join playwrighting groups and
volunteer to read new material. In Los Angeles, there is a
group of actors who have bound together to champion
animal rights. These groups not only provide another
avenue of association with your fellow actors, but they
supply a support group as well. Being involved in a
theater group or playreading group also looks good on
your resume. Take your place within the ranks of your
own profession.

The unions are as weak or as strong as the members. My own opinion is that there should be more stringent rules for membership that would take into consideration such things as training, apprenticeship and hours spent in the business. These types of rules govern craft unions such as hair and make-up.

Although it is difficult for a newcomer to join, there continue to be countless chronically non-working actors who are already union members. It is useless and expensive to join until you train yourself and have the tools (resume, craft and experience) to realistically expect employment.

When you join the union, vow to be an active, informed member. It's not always easy to obey rules others have made, so become involved and help make the rules. This is your profession. Take responsibility for your unions. It's important for working actors to become active members of their unions.

Wrap Up

✓ non-union jobs can provide film for your reel and growing credibility in the business if you are not yet a union member
✓ don't join until you are marketable
✓ working non-union hurts us all
✓ be an informed and active member

14 Get a Grip on Your Life

Before you commit yourself to any career, you need to know as much as possible about yourself and what you want. If you don't delineate who you are before you start chasing jobs, you not only won't have as much to sell, you may miss your opportunity to form yourself and end up as an empty vessel that only exists to be filled — by someone else.

Who knows? You might find you are somebody entirely different than you thought, to whom the unemployment or even employment might be less interesting than you thought.

Even though Mira Sorvino is the daughter of actor Paul Sorvino, her success has far eclipsed his, so she had no way of knowing what her success would cost.

✦   *"This summer was the first time I've taken off from work in five years, and I was able to reevaluate my life," she continued. "I thought about my grandfather, Poppy, who died in 1995 while I was making a movie. I missed his wake and his funeral because I couldn't get out of work. My LA life was so stacked up that way that I kept missing events that were happening in my real life."*

Sorvino hesitated a moment, and then said, "I've learned that the people I love, my real life have to be paramount. I learned I missed my wonderful friends and family, and I want to have my real life. I'm lucky knowing that."
What I Love Most
Dotson Rader
Parade Magazine
October 11, 1998

David Duchovny is surely happier now that *The X-files* has begun filming in Los Angeles, allowing Duchovny to pursue a real life again, but his candid remarks in an article in *Movieline* detail what it's really like to be the star of a successful television series. The reporter asked if he missed having a life:

✦ *I thought I did. I miss it desperately at this point. But when I went back to LA recently, I was shocked to find that I didn't have a life there, either. I mean, I'm okay, I can take care of myself. But I feel isolated and lonely. I'm not happy.*

Hiding in Plain Sight
Martha Frankel
Movieline
May 1997

The reporter asked Duchovny if he would have taken the series if he had known what it was going to be like:

✦ *Can I also know what it would have been like if I didn't take the series? I hate those kinds of things, where people say, 'Stop bitching, you could be working at Burger King now.' As if those are the only two options for me — either act or 'Would you like a soda with your fries?' I love acting, and I love* The X-Files. *But doing a television show is like riding an elephant — it goes where it wants, with or without your say. Does that make me an ungrateful bastard?*

Hiding in Plain Sight
Martha Frankel
Movieline
May 1997

Angelina Jolie made a big splash in 1998 in the highly acclaimed HBO movie, *Gia* and was also on display in the feature, *Playing by Heart*. She's another in a growing list who say it's not as they thought it would be:

✦ *I don't think I was ever more depressed in my life than the time I realized I was working in the business that I'd always wanted to be in; I was in love; I had money; and I wasn't struggling. I thought, 'Well, I have everything I'd always thought would make me really happy, and I don't feel okay.'*

Wild Angel
Tim Roston
Premiere
January 1999

Dan Hedaya is a well respected actor who has survived for years in the business. He only became visible when he played the father of Alicia Silverstone in the hit movie, *Clueless*. All of a sudden, he has job offers from every corner. Producers are even writing parts into their movies for the express purpose of hiring Dan. An article in *The New York Times* quoting Hedaya and others about his career, touched me greatly:

✦ *Mr. Hedaya is typical of any number of working actors, most of them with stage training, who are highly prized for their talents within the film and television business but not widely known outside it.*

"I wouldn't say I had years of struggle," said Mr. Hedaya, a disarmingly candid man who looks on his career with a blend of awe and amusement. "I was frustrated. I had lots of rejections. What actor doesn't? You get used to it."

....Scott Rudin, the producer who cast Hedaya in Clueless *met Hedaya years ago and was impressed with his believability before the camera.*

"Success has been really good for Dan. He went through a period of insecurity. He doubted for awhile that he would ever have the kind of career he wanted. For a while he was angry. He had an edge. He wanted the kind of career that guys like Bob Duvall or Harvey Keitel had, and never thought he would have one."

"I know brilliant actors who are struggling unbelievably hard," Hedaya said. "It breaks my heart. The rejection. The inability to get work. It can be so corrosive to the spirit. I know actors who live with this struggle every day. It's painful to watch. I've had good fortune. I'm working. That's what it's all about. All I do is look around me to realize how lucky I am."

Actor Fades Out of Anonymity
Bernard Weinraub
The New York Times
November 14, 1995

Sharon Stone isn't complaining, but the story of the life change when she became instantly famous is a little chilling:

◆   *I got famous from a Friday to a Tuesday. On Friday, I worked. On Tuesday, people were pounding on my car windows. Very shortly after that I went to Cannes for* Basic Instinct. *The roar never ceased, 24 hours a day for six days, to the point where, by the fifth day, I was on the floor in the bathroom of my friends' restaurant sweating and heaving.*

Dame Fame
Virginia Campbell
Movieline
June 1994

When Steven Jenkins left the business for a temporary job, he found there were other ways to get the validation he had sought from acting:

◆   *I'd been offered a guest artist contract at the University of Florida and, of course, just before I left, I'd given up my apartment, left my job, lost my girlfriend. So when I came back to New York — this was in '75 — I had no money, I had no prospects and I'd already been doing this acting for two years, which doesn't seem like a very long time, but when you're 22 it seems like an eternity.*

...so I got a job as a clerk. A year and a half later, I ended up at Dean & DeLuca and that's where it all started.

I was so knocked out that I was getting a paycheck every week and finally getting some responsibility. I wasn't freaking out every day about what I was going to do for my next anything. So I applied myself. I scrubbed, I rubbed, I swept. I showed up and I stayed late. I was going everything I could do to keep from turning tail and going back to my hometown.

America's Cheesemonger
Laurie Ochoa
The Los Angeles Times
February 12, 1997

Steve is an author and a internationally respected cheese expert at Dean & DeLuca in New York City.

Success

I've been in the business a long time and have watched the careers of many performers from rise to fall to rise again and I have witnessed the downside of money, fame and power. It costs a lot. Not just that your relationships with those near and dear to you may falter, but what it does to your body. Elevated status is stressful. Your whole physical being has to adjust. Carroll O'Connor told me that when *All in the Family* hit it big, that he was taking four Valium every day to try to calm himself down.

With elevated status comes power. You can misbehave without much repercussion. You can abuse people who have no recourse. If you have not learned early on to behave well because that is what is best for you in the long run, it's possible that you will lose control completely. Not only is it unconscionable to treat others badly, it will rot your soul and take its toll on you. You will have all those things you thought you wanted and still find your self in constant pain.

Finding Out More About Yourself

If you are 19 and play 13, you'd better get on with cashing in on that talent before you are too old. If you are exquisitely beautiful/handsome, perhaps you, too need to get to Hollywood, Chicago or New York right this minute.

Otherwise, if you have already finished your education, I suggest you take some time to get your bearing. Whenever I travel abroad, I am impressed that young people in other countries routinely finish at university and expect to spend a year traveling abroad.

Although there are many American colleges where *junior year abroad* is commonplace, not all colleges offer that option and most of us don't get the life enhancing experience of going to a strange place and improvising. Even if you have that opportunity, school is a protected environment that doesn't test your resources and spirit as does existing on your own.

A public relations woman I encountered in England told me she had spent a year in Australia before she set out to pursue her profession. She got temporary jobs here and there to make money and then traveled about.

A British scriptwriter I know, spent a year hosteling and backpacking in Australia before spending what turned out to be four years in Japan teaching English as a second language. During his time there, he taught himself how to write and saved money to come to the United States and sell himself as a scriptwriter.

He arrived not only with scripts in his bag, but a much richer imagination. He dedicates himself to writing every day. Several of his scripts have been optioned. He has made good American contacts by carefully selecting the creme of the crop in writing seminars around town. That's not only how I met him, but also how he met the producer who has optioned his scripts.

It's not just writers who need a store of experiences to nourish their art, actors need a vocabulary, too. No matter where you travel, if you are inventive, you can access the creative community.

Avril Thresh, a young British actress I met at The Court Theater in New Zealand had been doing theater in Glasgow when she met a man who said, *If you are ever in New Zealand, call me.*

Six months later, she was in Christchurch working at the theater as a stage manager, in the box office and as an actress. Her two month sojourn in NZ has not only turned into three years, but her parents came from Great Britain on holiday to visit her and immigrated to New Zealand permanently.

I'm not saying you're going to end up working as an actor or even in a theater related job, but just having that traveling experience will change your whole vision of the world.

I've come to traveling late in life. I always thought I was going to get a job and go on locations to exotic places like Julia Roberts does, and I did go to Spain on a job, but New Jersey has been more my speed.

It's only now that I realize that just like I don't have to wait for someone else to give me a job, I don't have to wait for someone else to create a job that will take me to another country. If I'm creative, I can take what I have and use it to travel and bond with other people in the business.

I was in New Zealand and Australia recently, and decided to do some research not only on the possibility of American actors getting work there, but also on how the natives go about getting work.

It looks like pursuing a job in any country, whether you live there or not, is an art in itself. To work your way into the system, you will just have to spend a certain amount of time not making any money. If you are going to study (a good way to get a card from immigration that would allow you to stay for a while), just as in the US, there are schools that have cache with the buyers.

New Zealand Schools & Production Centers

United Tech College of Performing Arts in Auckland, Toiwhakaari aka New Zealand Drama School in Wellington, and The National Academy of Singing and Dramatic Art (NASDA) in Christchurch are the schools of choice in New Zealand.

Peter Jackson (*Heavenly Creatures, The Frighteners*, and the upcoming *Lord of the Rings*) has been a big factor in Wellington being considered the film capital while there is more television work in Auckland where they film *Hercules* and *Xena*.

Christchurch sports The Court Theater, the most famous and credentialed theater in New Zealand, so that's the center for theater related jobs.

The lighting designer at The Court, Sheena Baines, told me she feels privileged to be working at the only theater in New Zealand with its own staff across the board. The Court is committed to producing New Zealand playwrights plus new foreign classics.

If you have teaching credentials and are interested in working in New Zealand, I would head for the library and do some research into universities and theaters. Sheena told me that an American actor who teaches stage fighting queried the Theater, was brought over to choreograph a particular show and has now immigrated to New Zealand and works their regularly.

Casting Directors in New Zealand

Do not fax pictures and resumes to casting directors unless requested. It is acceptable to fax a note indicating your interest in upcoming projects.

In order to work in any foreign country, you will need a work permit which will involve either a promise of work or a sponsor. If someone wants to hire you, they will usually help you find a sponsor.

As in any other market, the key to work is to involve yourself in activities that bring you in touch with people either already working in the business or close to it.

Casting director, Liz Mullane who is casting Peter Jackson's *Lord of the Rings* says it's probably not worth it for an actor to fly all the way to New Zealand just with the idea that he might get work. On the other hand, if you are in your year of experiencing life and happen to be in New Zealand, here is a list of their casting directors:

Terri De'ath	0-9-232-7818
Casting Link	fax 0-9-360-2180
300 Richmond Road	025-721-472
Ponsonby, Auckland, NZ	

Filed Rotes Casting Facility	
PO Box 6479	0-4-384-4540
Marion Square	fax 0-4-384-4540
Wellington, NZ	0-25-480-019

Simon Hughes
Marmalade Audio
PO Box 27266
Wellington, New Zealand
E-mail: marmalade_audio@compuserve.com
Website: http://www.marmalade.co.nz

0-4-385-9051
fax 0-4-385-4253

Andrea Kelland
PO Box 3421
Auckland,NZ
E-mail: andrea@centralcasting.co.nz

0-9-815-5585
fax 0-9-815-5542

Brenda Kendall
23 West View Road
Westmere, Auckland

0-9-376-3379
fax 0-9-376-3379

Liz Mullane Casting
18 Dean Street
Grey Lynn, Auckland, NZ

0-9-376-6918
fax 0-9-376-9079

Simon Marler
PO Box 3421
Auckland, NZ
E-mail: simon@centralcasting.co.nz

0-9-815-5585
fax 0-9-815-5542

Sally Meiklejohn
The Art Department Ltd.
PO Box 67111
Mt. Eden, Auckland, NZ
E-mail: artdept@ihug.co.nz

0-9-630-7007
fax 0-9-630-7007

Australian Work Opportunity

I interviewed Australian agent, Mark Morrissey who
told me that it is rare for an American actor to get work
there. The projects are Australian and buyers are looking
for Australians just as in America, where Australian
accents would only be needed for special projects.

Work for female actors is limited in Oz even more

than in the United States. Likewise mirroring the U.S. stats, there are more roles for women on television than in film as roles are more evenly divided between women and men in that media.

Morrissey said that American actors would be 75% less likely to get work since the Australian the accent is very subtle and difficult to copy

♦ *Even if you had decent American credits, you would still have to work yourself into the system, same as New York/Los Angeles.*
Mark Morrissey, agent
Sydney, Australia

In addition to getting chosen, you would have to procure a work visa. Check with the Australian Embassy to see what is required. Although you would need papers to work on an ongoing basis, papers are pretty easily come by that would allow enough work to keep you going on an extended holiday.

Travellers Contact Point

I happened across an amazing resource called Travellers Contact Point. TCP proves mail holding and forwarding, Travel Agent Services, Internet and computers with word processing capability. They also offer a job resource center.

When I checked the bulletin board, there were jobs for an au pair, a two week stint in airline reservations, a business consultant opportunity, work for farm workers and a job as a cook at a farmstay for three weeks. I was tempted to check that one out myself. It just sounded like a real adventure.

Their brochure advertises placements for legal, secretarial, sales and marketing, accounting, hospitality, travel, health care and trades.

TCP offers a Medicare card, insurance for your person as well as for loss of baggage, cameras, and other personal belongings and cancellation fees. You can be covered from a week to a year.

A personal E-mail address costs $10 a year and for $25 you can get a free address plus daily E-mail access.

Travellers Contact Point
Level 7/428 St. George St.
Sydney, Australia
02-9221-8744 fax: 02-9221-3746
E-mail: Sydney@travellers-contact.com.au

In Australia, TCP also has offices in Cairns and Perth. There is also a Travellers Contact Point Office in London

Travellers Contact Point
14 Barley Mow Passage
Cheswick, London
0181- 994 2247 fax: 0181-994 2269
E-mail: London@travellers.com.au

Cyberia Cafe in Dublin, Ireland in Temple Bar provides mail, resources and training. You can reach them at E-mail: info@cyberia.ie or 01-6797607.

There are similar cafes all over Ireland, Italy and most countries you can think if. Many only provide a place to write E-mail, but some provide either a job board or training. If you do a search (I used Infoseek and Yahoo), just type in Internet Cafes + country or city you want to research.

Hostelling International/The Y/Inexpensive Places to Stay

There are many inexpensive places to stay all over the world from the YWCA to youth and senior hostels and the Internet is a wealth of information about all of them.

Hostelling International is a non profit membership organization that promotes international understanding by bringing together travellers of all ages, backgrounds, and nationalities and represents more than 70 countries and 4.5 million members world wide.

Hostelling International membership provides access to nearly 200 hostels in the U.S. and 6,000 hostels worldwide. One year membership: $25.

Website: http://www.hiayh.org/ushostel/mdatreg/newyor.htm
Website: http://www.Hostelling.com.

Hostelling

Hostelling is called backpacking in many parts of the world and it's perhaps best described as travelling cheaply with an adventurous spirit. The terms hosteller and backpacker are basically synonymous.

In many countries, especially Australia and New Zealand, it's customary for students and recent graduates to take trips of up to a year or more!

While hostelling, you see the world from a perspective that the average tourist will never see. You meet local people, learn customs, eat local food and often have opportunities to do things you never imagined. Basically, backpackers stay longer, see more, and do more for less money.

The atmosphere at a hostel tends to be youthful, but people of all ages stay in them. Hostellers are usually outgoing, friendly and welcoming to newcomers. Hostels are an excellent place to stay for people travelling alone. Many solo travellers use hostels as a way of meeting others and sharing the travel experience.

At most hostels throughout the world there are no age restrictions. It is rumored that some hostels, such as some in Bavaria, will give priority to youths when the hostel is full.

hostel.com

I even found hostels in Los Angeles and New York.

Heart of Venice Beach
1515 Pacific Ave. (at Windward Ave)
Venice, CA 90291
310-452-3052/fax 310-821-3469
E-mail: vbh@caprica.com.

Len Brown
891 Amsterdam Avenue
New York, NY 10025-4403
212-932-2300
E-mail: hiayhnyc@aol.com

Many Ys offer rooms in the United States and overseas. For information on YMCA accommodations in the United States:

International Branch of the YMCA of Greater New York
71 W 23rd St. Suite 1904
New York, NY 10010
212-727-8800/fax: 212-727-8814

For specific country information on YMCA accommodations overseas:

800-872-9622.
Website: http://ymca.com/InterDir/intdir.htm

Be Careful What You Wish For

Good luck, remember, we are all one and there is enough for everyone. There's no need to despair and there is no need to worry. Will Rogers said, *We're all about as happy as we want to be*, and I'm sure we all arrive at the destination in the business that we choose. It's like Sharon Stone says: *Where you want to go is the important issue.* Take careful aim because you will get there.

Wrap Up

- ✓ discover yourself before you embark
- ✓ explore all avenues
- ✓ delineate your value system first
- ✓ everything costs
- ✓ test your resourcefulness
- ✓ travelling enlarges the actors vocabulary
- ✓ see what the opportunities are elsewhere
- ✓ be careful what you wish for

15   Glossary

Academy Players Directory — Catalogue of actors published three times a year for the Los Angeles market. It shows one or two pictures per actor and lists credits and representation. If you work freelance, you can list your name and service. Some list union affiliation. Casting directors, producers and whomever else routinely keeps track of actors use the book as a reference guide. Every actor who is ready to book should be in this directory. For forms and information, call 310-247-3000. New York counterpart is *The Players Guide*.

Actors' Unions — There are three: *Actors' Equity Association* (commonly referred to as Equity) is the union that covers actors employed in the theater. *American Federation of Television and Radio Artists* (commonly referred to as AFTRA) covers actors employed in videotape and radio. *Screen Actors Guild* (commonly referred to as SAG) covers actors employed in theatrical motion pictures and all product for television that is filmed.

Answering Services — Answering services come in many forms. The most expensive ones have a tie-in to your phone at home and, after a predesignated number of rings (when you haven't answered), they will pick up your line. Usually they announce themselves with your phone number or name. They note messages you receive and you call in for that information. The cheaper service has a central number you give to business contacts. You call in for your messages.

The alternative and what most people have these days is either Voice Mail or a good answering machine. Get one or the other the minute you hit town; actors cannot function without reliable telephone support. For years (paranoid soul that I am) I had a machine and a service. I guess the level of my anxiety is down because now I only have a machine.

There are any number of reputable answering services that exclusively represent actors. In Los Angeles, check *Backstage West* for ads; in New York check *ShowBusiness* and *Backstage*. Ask your friends about the services they use.

Audition Tape — Also known as a Composite Cassette Tape. This is a videotape showcasing either one performance or a montage of scenes of an actor's work, usually no longer than eight minutes and on VHS ½ inch. Agents and casting directors prefer to see tapes of professional appearances (film or television), but some will look at a tape produced for this purpose only.

Billing — The size and placement of your name in the credits of motion picture, film or television are negotiated along with your salary and is called billing and also delineates how many others are listed on same line (theater) or card (film or television).

Breakdown Service — Started in 1971 by Gary Marsh, the Service condenses scripts and lists parts available in films, television and theater. It is expensive and available to agents and managers only.

Buyer — This term refers to anyone on the road to your future employment, whether it be a casting executive, a writer, producer, director or an agent.

Call Back — After an initial reading, ranks of auditioners are reduced and the best are *called back* to read again. This can go on for days.

Clear — The unions demand that the agent check with a freelance actor (clearing) before submitting him on a particular project.

Cold or Cold Readings — Reading a script aloud at an audition with no chance to study ahead of time is always a bad idea and is called a *cold read*. Some acting schools teach what are called Cold Reading Workshops. I have never understood the value. In my 30-year career, I have rarely been called upon to read a script instantly on first viewing, except at commercials where it's a good idea to arrive early, pick up the copy, and head for the bathroom so they won't call you in until you are ready.

Composite Cassette Tape — See Audition Tape.

Contact Sheets — An 8x10 proof sheet printed by your photographer displaying all the pictures he took of you. Different photographers make different arrangements, but usually the photographer takes at least two rolls of film and you get two different 8x10 prints. The photographer delivers these to you and it is up to you to find an inexpensive place to get these pictures duplicated.

Credits — List of roles the actor has played.

Dailies — Viewing by producers, directors and crew of all film shot the day before, in order to evaluate performances, lighting, make-up, etc. Actors are frequently not allowed to attend.

Equity-Waiver Productions — See Showcases.

Freelance — The term used to describe the relationship between an actor and agent or agents who submit the actor for work without an exclusive contract. New York agents frequently will work on this basis; Los Angeles agents rarely consent to this arrangement.

Going Out — Auditions or meetings with directors and/or casting directors. These are usually set up by your agent, but have also been set up by very persistent and courageous actors.

Gopher — Term used to describe all-around errand person on a set (or office) who goes for whatever anyone needs (i.e., errands, coffee, etc).

Guesting — Appearing in one or more episodes of a television show. This term is used to differentiate from those actors who are contracted to appear in all or a major portion of the shows.

Hot — Show-biz talk for actor who is currently in great demand.

Industrials — Industrial shows are splashy Broadway-type musicals produced by and for big business to sell their wares. They pay more than Broadway. The most famous is Monsanto in New York. There are also industrial films.

Interview — A meeting with a casting director, producer, writer, agent or director. This is different from an audition, because, in an audition, you read for the buyer.

Letter of Termination — A legal document dissolving the contract between actor and agent. If you decide to leave your agent while your current contract is in effect, it is usually possible to do so citing Paragraph 6 of the SAG Agency Regulations. Paragraph 6 allows either the actor or the agent to terminate the contract, if the actor has not worked for more than 15 of the previous 91 days, by sending a letter of termination.

Dear:

This is to inform you that, relative to Paragraph 6 of the Screen Actors Basic Contract, I am terminating our contract as of this date.

Send a copy of the letter to your agent via registered mail, return receipt requested. Also send a copy to the Screen Actors Guild and all other unions involved. Retain a copy for your files.

Major Role/Top of the Show — A predetermined fee set by producers which, in most cases, is a non-negotiable maximum for guest appearances on television episodes.

See minimums.

Mark — The term used when rehearsing for the camera. You walk through the scene to show the cinematographer and his crew where you will be moving. This movement is determined by the director.

Equity Minimum — The least amount of money per day that an Equity member may work for without special permission from the union. See Chapter 13 for details.

AFTRA Minimum — The least amount of money per day that an AFTRA member may work for without special permission from the union. AFTRA has two different sets of minimums for their players: day rates and nighttime rates. See Chapter 13 for details.

Screen Actors Guild Minimum — The least amount of money that a SAG member can work for without special permission from the union. See Chapter 13 for details.

Money — Beginning actors work for minimum. As your career progresses, your price goes up relative to your power. Money refers to the largest amount of money you have been paid to date for a day, week, series, etc. See also *Quote*.

Open Calls — Refer to auditions or meetings held by casting directors that are not set up by agents. No individual appointments are given. Usually the call is made in an advertisement in one of the trade newspapers, by flyers or in a news story in the popular press.

As you can imagine, the number of people that show up is enormous. You will have to wait a long time. Although management's eyes tend to glaze over and see nothing after a certain number of hours, actors do sometimes get jobs this way.

Option — Someone pays money to exclusively control a property or a person's services in a particular category for a period of time. Sometimes the option expires without the project coming to fruition.

Overexposed — Term used by nervous buyers (producers, networks, casting directors, etc.) indicating an actor has become too recognizable for their tastes. Maybe he just got off a situation comedy and everyone remembers him as a particular character. The buyer doesn't want the public thinking of that instead of his project. A thin line exists between not being recognizable and being overexposed.

Per Diem — Negotiated amount of money for expenses on location or on the road per day.

Pictures — The actor's calling card. An 8x10 glossy black and white photograph.

Pilot — The first episode of a proposed television series. Produced so that the network can determine whether there will be additional episodes. There are many pilots made every year. Few go to series. Fewer stay on the air for more than a single season.

Players Guide — Catalogue of actors published annually for the New York market. It lists one or two pictures per actor plus credits and representation. Actors list union affiliation if they choose. If you work freelance, you can list your name and service. Casting directors, producers and whomever else routinely keeps track of actors use the book as a reference guide. You must be a member of one of the performer's unions to be included. Every actor who is ready to book should be in this directory. Their number is 212-302-9497. Los Angeles equivalent is *The Academy Players Directory*.

Principal — Job designation indicating a part larger than an extra or an *Under Five*.

Product — For the actor, the product is himself.

Process — People are continually talking about the process. This refers to the ongoing mechanisms involved in developing our personas, careers and/or the rehearsal procedure in a play.

Property — Refers to book, play, story, film that has been acquired for development, production and/or distribution.

Quote — The most highest negotiated sum an actor was able to command for a particular job. Don't lie. They will check.

Ready to Book — Agent talk for an actor who has been trained and judged mature enough to handle himself in auditions, not only with material, but also with buyers. This frequently refers to an actor whose progress in acting class or theater has been monitored by the agent.

Resume — The actor's ID; lists credits, physical description, agent's name and phone contact.

Right — When someone describes an actor as being right for a part, he is speaking about the essence of an actor. We all associate a particular essence with Jim Carrey and a different essence with Brad Pitt. One would not expect Carrey and Pitt to be up for the same part. Being right also involves credits. The more important the part, the more credits are necessary to support being seen.

Rollcall — The information age version of *The Players Guide* and *The Academy Players Directory*. Information is fed into subscribers' computers. The advantage is you can update your resume as often as you like. There are differing opinions about this service. Some agents think it's stupid. I don't see the harm. It doesn't cost that much to be listed and many important buyers subscribe.

Roughcut — First piecing together of film, usually without music, effects, etc.

Scale — See minimums.

Scale Plus 10 — When a job only pays scale, in order for the actor to actually take home scale (which the union demands), the deal is made for scale plus 10% so that the agent's commission is not taken from the actor's pay. That means if an agent negotiates, he must negotiate his own 10%. If you had negotiated for yourself, you would only have gotten scale.

Seen — Term referring to an actor's having had an interview or audition and being considered for a part.

Showcases — Productions in which members of Actors' Equity are allowed by the union to work without compensation are called *Showcases* in New York and *Equity Waiver* or *99-Seat Theater Plan* in Los Angeles. Equity members are allowed to perform as long as the productions conform to certain Equity guidelines: rehearsal conditions, expense reimbursement, limiting number of performances and seats, providing a set number of complimentary tickets for industry people. The producers must provide tickets for franchised agents, casting directors and producers.

Sides — The pages of script called sides contain just the scenes to be used for the audition. This is usually not enough information to use as a source to do a good audition. If they won't give you a complete script, go early (or the day before), sit in the office and read it. SAG rules require producers to allow actors access to the script (if it's written).

Stage Time — Term used to designate the amount of time a performer has had in front of an audience.

Most agents and casting executives believe that an actor can only achieve a certain level of confidence by amassing stage time. They're right.

Submissions — Sending an actor's name to a casting director in hopes of getting the actor an audition or meeting for a part.

Take — Cinematic term used to describe a scene when the camera is rolling that is chosen to be printed.

Talent — Management's synonym for actors.

Top of the Show — A pre-determined fee set by producers which is a non-negotiable maximum for guest appearances on television episodes. This is also referred to as *Major Role Designation*.

The Trades — *Variety* and *The Hollywood Reporter* are usually referred to as *The Trades*, although *Backstage* and *ShowBusiness* (in New York) and *Backstage West* (in Los Angeles) are also showbiz newspapers listing information about classes, auditions, casting, etc. These publications are particularly helpful to newcomers. All are available at good newsstands or by subscription.

Under Five — An AFTRA job in which the actor has five or fewer lines. This is paid at a specific rate — less than a principal and more than an extra. This scale is only part of the AFTRA contract, not SAG.

Visible/Visibility — Currently on view in film, theater or television. In this business, it's out of sight, out of mind, so visibility is very important.

99-Seat Theater Plan — The Los Angeles version of the *Showcase*, originally called *Waiver*. Producers give actors expense compensation of $5-$14 per performance. It's not much, but it adds up; at least you're not working for free. Producers must also conform to Equity guidelines regarding rehearsal conditions, number of performances, complimentary tickets for industry, etc. If you participate in this plan, be sure to stop by Equity and get a copy of your rights.

Indexes

Index to Agents

Index to Comedy Clubs & Their Owners

Index to People

Index to Resources

Index to Everything Else